Wyatt Earp

Legends of the Wild West

Sitting Bull

Billy the Kid

Calamity Jane

Buffalo Bill Cody

Crazy Horse

Davy Crockett

Wyatt Earp

Geronimo

Wild Bill Hickok

Jesse James

Nat Love

Annie Oakley

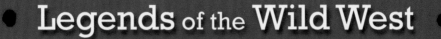

Wyatt Earp

Adam Woog

CHELSEA HOUSE
PUBLISHERS
An imprint of Infobase Publishing

For my father, a cowboy at heart all his life.

Wyatt Earp

Copyright © 2010 by Infobase Publishing

Chelsea House
An imprint of Infobase Publishing
132 West 31st Street
New York NY 10001

Library of Congress Cataloging-in-Publication Data
Woog, Adam, 1953-
 Wyatt Earp / by Adam Woog.
   p. cm. — (Legends of the wild West)
 Includes bibliographical references and index.
 ISBN 978-1-60413-597-8 (hardcover)
 1. Earp, Wyatt, 1848-1929—Juvenile literature. 2. Peace officers—Southwest, New—Biography—Juvenile literature. 3. United States marshals—Southwest, New—Biography—Juvenile literature. 4. Southwest, New--Biography—Juvenile literature. 5. Tombstone (Ariz.)—History—19th century—Juvenile literature. I. Title.
 F786.E18W66 2010
 978'.02092—dc22
 [B]   2009035969

Chelsea House books are available at special discounts when purchased in bulk quantities for businesses, associations, institutions, or sales promotions. Please call our Special Sales Department in New York at (212) 967-8800 or (800) 322-8755.

You can find Chelsea House on the World Wide Web at
http://www.chelseahouse.com

Text design by Kerry Casey
Cover design by Keith Trego
Composition by EJB Publishing Services
Cover printed by Bang Printing, Brainerd, MN
Book printed and bound by Bang Printing, Brainerd, MN
Date printed: February 2010
Printed in the United States

10 9 8 7 6 5 4 3 2 1

This book is printed on acid-free paper.

All links and Web addresses were checked and verified to be correct at the time of publication. Because of the dynamic nature of the Web, some addresses and links may have changed since publication and may no longer be valid.

CONTENTS

WYATT EARP'S EARLY LIFE

"It's all true, give or take a lie or two."

—*James Garner as Wyatt Earp*
in the 1988 movie Sunset

Wyatt Earp is one of the most famous figures to emerge from the wild and woolly place known as the Old West. He is best remembered today as a lawman, especially for his role in a legendary shootout. This shootout, known as the Gunfight at the O.K. Corral, was key in establishing Earp's reputation as a tough and daring peace officer in a time and place where there was often precious little law enforcement—and where informal justice could be swift and violent. But upholding the law was only one facet of this complex man's colorful career. In fact, he was a marshal for only a few of his 81 years.

Over the course of his long life, Earp was also a farmer, stagecoach driver, railroad laborer, buffalo hunter, gambler, saloonkeeper, miner, and boxing referee. Historian Paula Mitchell Marks, in her book *And Die in the West,* calls Earp's working life "a dizzying array of frontier occupations."

Wyatt Earp had many occupations, working as a gambler, a saloon keeper, a boxing referee, a gold and copper miner, and a lawman. Due to his fondness for storytelling, he became known as the toughest and deadliest gunman in the Old West.

The variety of jobs he held was typical for men of Earp's time and place, where people did whatever they had to do to survive, and few occupations, by themselves, could support them. But it is

Earp's exploits as a peace officer, however, that made him famous. His larger-than-life personality and his love of telling stories about himself—many of them liberally exaggerated—helped cement his legend. As a result, historian Allen Barra notes in his book *Inventing Wyatt Earp*, "Every American knows the name of Wyatt Earp."

A LIFELONG TRAVELING MAN

There are other reasons besides necessity for Earp's wide-ranging career. One is that he inherited from his father a restless nature, a need to be on the move nearly all the time. For essentially his entire adult life, Earp was a traveling man, always trying his hand at new livelihoods.

This lifelong habit is an apt symbol for frontier life. The Old West was a place of swift changes, abrupt movement, vast spaces, and unpredictability. The frontier thus presented a perfect environment for someone like Earp who was prone to restlessness and traveling. This world also easily lent itself to the very American notion that it is possible to re-invent oneself completely, that people need not be limited to a single job or a single place—a notion that clearly appealed to Earp.

Another reason behind Earp's varied career is that he was a notoriously confrontational character. He refused to bow down to authority, could be brusque and humorless, and as a deputy lawman sometimes dealt with outlaws in ways that today would be considered brutal. None of these qualities endeared him to employers, and unhappy bosses often urged him to move on.

There is a third, more mundane reason why Earp worked at so many jobs: Being a lawman in the Old West was rarely a full-time job. Most of Earp's lawman career took place in cattle towns, those end points for the era's massive cattle drives. Teams of men, called drovers (and later more generally called cowboys), brought huge numbers of cattle north over hundreds of miles along dusty trails from Texas. Their destinations were typically railway centers in Oklahoma and Kansas. The cattle were then shipped by train to markets in the East.

These cattle drives were usually the busiest and most lucrative times of the year in the rough and ready cattle towns of the West. They were annual events, almost always occuring in late summer or early autumn. At other times of year, when the drovers were not in town, things were generally quiet. Life was slow, with relatively little crime beyond the occasional horse theft or drunken brawl.

When the drovers arrived, however, town life changed dramatically. After they had finished their long, demanding, and dusty journeys, the drovers had plenty of cash, plenty of free time, and plenty of opportunity to partake of the drinking, gambling, and female companionship they had missed while on the trail.

Furthermore, the cowboys—indeed, virtually every man in the Old West—openly carried guns. This was standard practice for the time, when weapons were necessary for survival. The combination of money and time to spend and plentiful weaponry created a perfect recipe for trouble. Thus, for much of the year, there was little need for peacekeeping, but when the drovers were in town, the crime rate skyrocketed.

Being a peace officer was therefore seasonal work. Men like Earp had no guarantee of year-round employment as deputies, marshals, or sheriffs. In the off seasons, they took on other jobs such as farming, ranching, prospecting, or gambling.

These part-time or temporary jobs were not always completely legal. Though never proved, for instance, there is some evidence that Earp occasionally acted outside of the law. Many of the alleged incidents—but not all of them—took place before he became a lawman. Among other crimes, Earp was accused at various times of such unsavory activities as horse theft and embezzlement.

For most of Earp's colorful life, he was unknown beyond a relatively small group of people. Within this group he was a respected—and sometimes feared—man, but he was hardly the celebrity he would become later in life. (In fact, his older brother Virgil was for many years much better known.) Wyatt Earp was just another man trying to make his way in a rough environment. This path began in the days when he was just a boy.

NICK EARP

Wyatt Earp's father was Nicholas Porter Earp, often called Nick. Nick had been born in North Carolina in 1813, but he grew up in Kentucky. The family name is apparently of Scottish-English origin. Some researchers think it may be a variation of Harp.

Nick Earp's first wife, whom he married in 1836, was Abigail Storm, a native of Kentucky. They had two children, a boy named Newton and a girl named Mariah. Abigail Earp died in 1839, just two months after giving birth to Mariah. Eight months later, baby Mariah also died. Serious illness or death for infants, or for mothers who had recently given birth, was all too common in those days before antibiotics and other medical advances.

Nick was now a widower with a two-year-old son to care for. He quickly sought a new wife to share his burden, and he remarried about a year after Abigail's death. His new bride was Virginia Ann (Ginnie Ann) Cooksey, who was, like her husband, a native of North Carolina.

They were wed in Kentucky in 1840 and Nick fathered eight more children, most of whom lived into adulthood. They were, in order of birth, James, Virgil, Martha, Wyatt, Morgan, Warren, Virginia, and Adelia.

Shortly before Wyatt's birth, Nick Earp gave way to the restless nature that would characterize him and much of his family for many years. In *Inventing Wyatt Earp*, Barra comments, "The strange odyssey of Nicholas' life would cover nearly 8,000 miles [12,874 kilometers] by wagon and railroad over four decades." He took Ginnie Ann, along with Newton, James, Virgil, and Martha, away from Kentucky. They were originally bound for California, but they got no farther than the Midwest, where they settled in the farming community of Monmouth, Illinois.

Monmouth was a small town with a population of about 1,000. Nick's brother had once visited the region, and he recommended it to Nick. Nick liked it, too, and decided it would be a good place in which to raise his young and growing family. He found a variety of work around Monmouth. He was a cooper (barrel maker), a real-estate broker, a storekeeper, and a farmer of wheat, corn, and tobacco.

He also served as a third sergeant in the Illinois Mounted Volunteers during the Mexican-American War (1846–1848), which was sparked when the United States annexed Texas from Mexico. The U.S. victory in this conflict led to a huge region of what is now the American Southwest being surrendered to the States.

THE BIRTH OF WYATT EARP

Nick was sent home early from the war because of a leg injury suffered when a mule kicked him. After Nick's return, the most famous of the Earp children was born.

Wyatt Berry Stapp Earp was born in Monmouth on March 19, 1848. He was named in honor of his father's commanding officer during the war, Captain Wyatt Berry Stapp, whom Nick greatly admired. The Earps and their new baby did not stay long in Monmouth, moving in March 1849 when Wyatt was only a year old.

The Earps' new home was a 160-acre (65 hectare) farm seven miles (11 km) northeast of Pella, Iowa. The government had granted this land to Nick for his service during the war. Helped by Ginnie Ann and their older children, Nick began to farm his newly acquired property, planting corn and other crops. He found other forms of work in Pella, including repairing horse harnesses and serving as a notary public and a justice of the peace. Notary publics typically were responsible for witnessing the signing of important documents, while justices of the peace served as judges in legal cases and oversaw enforcement of the law.

In serving as a justice of the peace, Nick continued a family tradition: His father, Walter Earp, had been a justice of the peace in Kentucky.

WYATT'S BOYHOOD

As he grew up in Pella, Wyatt was a typically active and energetic boy. Like his brothers and sisters, he was expected to help out for much of each day with the many chores around the home and farm. Wyatt quickly discovered that he hated the hard work and long hours that were a necessary part of life on a farm. The only good thing about farm work, as far as he was concerned, was that it allowed him to spend time around horses. Being able to ride well was a source of pride to the boy. It was also a necessity: Horses or horse-drawn vehicles were the only means of transportation across the vast, sparsely settled regions of the Midwest.

Riding also gave Wyatt the opportunity to hunt and use firearms, activities he thoroughly enjoyed. Handling guns, like riding a horse, was a common—even necessary—practice for boys in the West. Wyatt became an excellent shot. Riding and hunting gave him the freedom to roam the countryside—at least in the little spare time that remained after his chores were finished.

The Earps remained in Pella for several years. Then, in 1856, Nick got restless again. He sold the farm and moved his family back to Monmouth. While he was unable to find sufficient work there at the kinds of manual labor that he had done in the past, he was elected Monmouth's deputy sheriff.

Once again this job did not last long. In the late 1850s, Nick traveled to California by himself, hoping to find a good location for farming. He liked San Bernardino County, and he returned to Monmouth to collect his family and make the move west. But the trip was delayed when his daughter Martha became ill and died.

Nick resumed his duties as a deputy sheriff. He also had a sideline business that would seem to be at odds with maintaining the law: He made and sold bootleg liquor. This job made him unpopular among many of the citizens of Monmouth. They pressured town authorities to arrest Nick, and in 1859 he was tried, convicted, and fined. When he could not pay the fine, the family was forced to sell its land and many of its belongings. The Earps again pulled up stakes and returned to Pella.

THE CIVIL WAR BREAKS OUT

Over the course of the next year, Nick revisited Monmouth several times. He had to finish overseeing the sale of his properties and settle several lawsuits pending against him involving debts he had incurred and accusations of tax evasion.

Nick still hoped to move his family to California. In 1860, however, a catastrophe not only delayed their plans but dramatically changed the course of life for the entire nation. This disruption, of course, was the Civil War, in which the Southern states tried to break away and form a separate nation, the Confederate States of America.

Although the reasons for the long and bloody conflict were complex, slavery was the primary issue. The South was strongly in favor of maintaining slavery, in large part because it needed massive amounts of cheap labor to keep its cotton plantations solvent. Meanwhile, the North (also known as the Union) was equally passionate about abolishing slavery throughout all the states.

The issue of slavery did not divide just the nation into warring factions but, frequently, even family members were at odds. This split in loyalty occurred in Wyatt's family. In 1861, the three oldest Earp boys, Newton, James, and Virgil, volunteered to be soldiers in the Union Army. Their father, in many ways, remained sympathetic to the goals of the Confederacy, which included Nick's native Kentucky. Yet, not only did he did not object to his sons fighting for the Union, during much of the war Nick helped recruit and train companies of local army volunteers for the Union forces. Perhaps his loyalty to his Southern roots was weakened by several years of life in the North.

The three Earp brothers served their country well. James was badly wounded in battle and was forced to return to the family farm in the summer of 1863. Newton and Virgil escaped injury, took part in several battles, and returned when the war ended in 1865.

During the war years, the other three Earp boys, Wyatt, Morgan, and Warren, were far too young to fight. Because they had to stay at home, and because their father was often busy elsewhere, they shouldered much of the responsibility for maintaining the family farm. Nonetheless, according to legend, despite his youth Wyatt tried several times to run away and join the military. In each case, his father found him and brought him home. Wyatt may have exaggerated these stories of his attempts to run away to fight, however.

ON TO CALIFORNIA

In time, with all of his boys back home, Nick was finally able to move his family from the Midwest. They were again bound for California—Nick's original destination and the place he had been to before his daughter Martha died. The Earps joined a small wagon train that was heading toward the West Coast. This train was typical of the day in which 20 or more horse-drawn vehicles crossed the frontier in groups to protect themselves and offer mutual assistance.

There is no solid evidence that Wyatt Earp ever returned to the Midwest of his youth. According to John Flood, an early biographer of Earp, the lawman returned to Illinois as an adult to revisit his old home there; however, this story hasn't been verified. Like so many anecdotes about Earp, it has probably been exaggerated over the years. In any case, Barra, in *Inventing Wyatt Earp: His Life and Many Legends*, reprints Flood's assertion that Earp was nostalgic for his childhood home—and then disappointed at what he found:

> The dear old Monmouth [he saw now] was not the Monmouth as he had remembered it; everything had changed. The great, high fences that he had to climb up to look over when he was a boy seemed dwarfed and shrunken now. . . . [T]he woods and fields were not the great, unexplored horizons that they used to be. The rivers and streams seemed narrow and diminutive [very small], and the rolling hills had lost their enchantment."

Adventures En Route

The family apparently had a number of memorable experiences on the way to California. For example, Wyatt later related that he hunted buffalo with the famous trapper and explorer Jim Bridger and

On May 12, 1864, the Earp family joined a wagon train headed to California. During their travels, the Earps reportedly encountered Paiute Indians near Fort Laramie, and Wyatt hunted buffalo with the famous scout Jim Bridger. Researchers have been unable to find evidence to confirm these stories.

claimed that the family encountered hostile Native Americans near Fort Laramie, Wyoming.

Wyatt's nephew, Bill Miller, told one biographer that the Earp family had had a run-in with a member of the Paiute tribe on the journey. According to Miller, the Paiute man had been hanging around the Earp campfire when Nick lost his temper and kicked the unwelcome visitor in the seat of his pants. As noted in Barra's *Inventing Wyatt Earp*, Miller stated that Wyatt said,

> I was expecting trouble and got my gun as soon as we saw this Indian, who'd been hanging around begging and probably trying to steal and generally making a nuisance of himself. He wasn't the only one.

I stood out of the way behind a wagon. He pulled a knife and Pa pulled a six-shooter and I would have shot him if he hadn't put his knife away and left. I had him covered and come close to shooting, except that Pa got in the way. If he'd have got Pa, I aimed to cut him down. I had a six-shooter in my belt and could have stood the ten others off. There wasn't a one of them with any sand [courage] if you stood up to them, but they all had mean tempers and they were all thieves.

There is no hard evidence to support this and most of the other stories about this journey, however. Overeager biographers of Earp—and Earp himself—may well have invented them.

In any case, the journey apparently awakened or fostered the young man's appetite for excitement. Writer Stuart Lake, another early biographer, is quoted in this regard in Barra's *Inventing Wyatt Earp*: "[T]he taste of life he had enjoyed during the covered wagon journey made him loathe to return to books [and] by spring he had set his own mind definitely against any vocation [job] that might hold him from adventuring."

Even if the Earps did not have such exciting experiences as legend would have it, traveling by wagon train was surely a long, difficult, and often dangerous adventure. In addition to Native American tribes, who were typically hostile toward white settlers, there were many other hazards: disease and starvation, treacherous rivers and mountains, the freezing cold of winter and the fierce heat of baking deserts. Nonetheless, the entire family survived.

When they finally reached California, the Earps settled near San Bernardino. At the time, San Bernardino was a boomtown—that is, a town that was growing rapidly around some sort of sudden wealth, such as a gold strike. At the time, San Bernardino had about 2,000 people. In comparison, nearby Los Angeles was just a tiny and dusty village.

The Earps' new home was full of life and activity, and the growing Earp boys were virtually guaranteed jobs. In *Inventing Wyatt*

The discovery of minerals like gold, silver, and copper led thousands of pioneers to go west in search of riches. The rapid population increase led to the creation of boomtowns, or communities that experience sudden growth. San Bernardino in southern California, where the Earps lived, and San Francisco, in northern California (*pictured above during the gold rush*) are examples of boomtowns.

Earp, Barra says of San Bernardino, "Prospectors, hunters, cattlemen, lumberjacks, soldiers and freighters [men who transported freight] filled the streets; a husky teenager might have his pick from a variety of jobs."

By the summer of 1865, 17-year-old Wyatt and his older brothers had a variety of jobs. Wyatt and Virgil first found work driving for a stagecoach line in California's Imperial Valley. The work suited them: Both young men liked being around horses, and both liked to travel.

According to some sources, Wyatt drank whiskey for the first time during this period. He felt so sick afterward, however, that he avoided alcohol for the next 20 years—indulging only very moderately. His friend Bill Tilghman, quoted in Barra's *Inventing Wyatt Earp,* recalled, "In all the years during which I was intimately associated with Wyatt, as a buffalo hunter and a peace officer, I never knew him to take a drink of liquor."

Earp also worked hauling supplies for railroad construction crews and became a teamster, the original term for men who transported goods on wagons drawn by horses, mules, or oxen. The new job gave Wyatt the opportunity to travel more widely. One of his routes took him from Wilmington, California, to Prescott in what was then Arizona Territory. He also worked along a route from San Bernardino through Las Vegas, in what was then Nevada Territory, and onward to Salt Lake City, Utah. Wyatt's job as a teamster did not last long. In 1868, he accompanied the rest of the Earps back to the Midwest. This time they settled in another small town: Lamar, Missouri. There, Nick resumed his work in maintaining law and order by becoming the town constable, or sheriff.

"LAWBREAKERS HAD BETTER WATCH OUT"

Wyatt soon followed in his father's footsteps and became an officer of the law. Nick was appointed Lamar's justice of the peace late in 1869. Wyatt then ran for the job of constable and took his father's place.

His oldest brother, Newton, was one of several others running against Wyatt. Some historians have suggested that the brothers deliberately competed in order to improve the odds that one Earp would get the job. Whether or not this is true, Wyatt beat his brother. Various sources cite a victory margin of either 29 or 35 votes, out of a total of about 100. The contest apparently caused no friction between the brothers, since Newton later named one of his children after Wyatt.

With Nick serving as justice of the peace and Wyatt working as the sheriff, the Earp family had the business of enforcing the law in the town neatly sewn up. Upon Wyatt's election to the job, a local newspaper, as cited in Barra's *Inventing Wyatt Earp*, commented, "This is a good appointment, and when our city dads get the machine in grinding order lawbreakers had better watch out."

And thus it was that the sleepy little town of Lamar, Missouri, was where the most famous lawman in the Old West got his first taste of the job that would soon make him a legend.

BECOMING
A LAWMAN

Earp's work as a law officer in Lamar was relatively easy. There was little crime beyond the occasional drunken cowboy who required jailing until he sobered up. Historian Casey Tefertiller, in his book *Wyatt Earp: The Life Behind the Legend*, comments, "The biggest controversy Earp faced as constable was a civic dispute over whether the lawman should be responsible for herding away hogs that ran loose on the street."

But Earp's time in Lamar was eventful in other ways—in particular, his private life took significant turns. In the summer of 1870 he bought a house and land for $50 (roughly $1,000 in today's money). He probably made this purchase because he got married. His bride, Urilla Sutherland, was the daughter of a local hotelkeeper. Earp's father, in his capacity as justice of the peace, performed the ceremony.

Tragically, the marriage was short-lived. Urilla died less than a year after the wedding. Sources differ on the cause of her death, but it was likely due either to typhus or complications in childbirth. Both were often deadly in the days before modern medicine—especially in relatively remote outposts like Lamar.

A CLOUD OF SUSPICION

In addition to his young wife's death, Earp faced a number of other unhappy events during this period. Notable among these was that he was forced to resign as constable under a cloud of suspicion after the county filed a lawsuit against him. The charge was embezzlement—specifically, of failing to deliver money that had been collected for license fees intended to support local schools. Earp was further accused of pocketing other funds that should have gone to the local court.

Not long after his wife's death and the loss of his job, Earp sold his land and house. He left Lamar and drifted to what was known as the Indian Territory, in present-day Oklahoma. But Earp ran into trouble there as well and was charged with several crimes. The most serious of the charges came when he and two other men were arrested for horse stealing. Horses were an essential part of life in the Old West, so such theft was a serious offense. Marks cites in *And Die in the West* one pioneer's comment: "In those early days human life didn't count for much. It seemed nothing to shoot a man down, but if anyone stole a horse he could expect to be hung if caught."

It is not clear if Earp was guilty. In any case, he and another of the accused men posted a $500 bond late in 1871—and Earp promptly disappeared. An arrest warrant was issued for him, but the charges were eventually dropped.

The young man's apparent criminal tendencies did not bode well for his future. It is possible that at this stage of his life Earp might have become a career criminal. Marks writes in *And Die in the West*, "[I]t seems likely that 23-year-old Wyatt Earp nearly found himself bound for a career that would have landed him inside a jail instead of guarding one."

PEORIA, ILLINOIS

For the several years after he skipped bond in the Indian Territory, Earp's whereabouts remain largely uncertain. There is evidence that he spent some time hunting buffalo in Kansas and wandering elsewhere around the Great Plains.

Despite this uncertainty over his general whereabouts, it is known that Earp lived for a time in Peoria, Illinois, a prosperous town on the Illinois River. His brother Virgil had once worked there as a saloonkeeper. Presumably, he recommended the town to Wyatt, who with another Earp brother, Morgan, moved there in the early 1870s.

The Earps are listed in the city directory for Peoria of 1872. The directory states that they lived in a brothel run by a woman named Jane Haspel. This is borne out by police records indicating that on three occasions authorities raided Haspel's house, where among those arrested were both Earp boys.

The authorities were not pleased. The Peoria police convicted and fined the brothers on at least one occasion for "keeping and being found in a house of ill-fame." Nevertheless, Wyatt continued to live in Haspel's house despite his arrests. It is likely that he also helped run another brothel, this one on a boat moored on the Illinois River.

Up to this point, Earp had no clear idea of what profession to follow. He had tried his hand at a number of jobs but was never satisfied with any of them. Earp had spent some time as a buffalo hunter, and he apparently still considered himself one. The enormous buffalo herds of the Western frontier had long provided a good living for thousands of hunters. A skilled hunter could kill as many as 250 animals in a single day and sell their hides.

The animals' hides were generally shipped back east to be made into coats and other goods. Buffalo meat, meanwhile, was sometimes used as food by army troops, though more often than not the animals' carcasses were simply left to rot on the open prairie once their valuable hides had been taken.

Now, however, these animals—which had once numbered in the tens of millions—were being killed off so rapidly that they were in serious danger of extinction. The prairies were strewn with the bare skeletons of buffalo killed for their hides, and only a few

As more and more people headed west, the amount of buffalo was reduced as settlers hunted down the animal for its hide and meat. Once numbering about 40 million, by 1889 the buffalo was nearly extinct, reduced to fewer than 500. Thanks to government legislation and the actions of private groups, today there are more than 350,000 buffalo in North America.

thousand of the creatures remained. The days of making a good living as a buffalo hunter were coming to an end.

Meanwhile, other forms of commerce were opening up, spurred on by reliable rail lines that were steadily being extended across the West. The efficiency of transportation via these railroads resulted in the ever-expanding number and growth of cattle towns. The lines also made it possible for boomtowns to grow up around such phenomena as silver and gold strikes.

These lively boomtowns of the frontier promised plenty of work for all—and plenty of excitement, which always appealed to Earp. The young man, by now in his mid-twenties, decided it was time to retire from buffalo hunting and seek his future in other ways. So he sold his buffalo gun and set out for Wichita, Kansas, in the late fall of 1874.

Wichita was one of the major hubs for the cattle drives coming up from Texas. Like most boomtowns, it had sprung up seemingly overnight, and it was a dramatic sight looming up from the flat, almost featureless landscape of the Midwest. As Tefertiller writes in *Wyatt Earp: The Life Behind the Legend*, "From the horizon, Wichita seemed to rise from a sea of grass on the prairie, a collection of buildings straddling the banks of the Arkansas River."

EVERYTHING GOES IN WICHITA

Some of these buildings in Wichita housed practical businesses: stores selling a variety of supplies, for example, or hotels where weary drovers could find baths and beds after weeks on the trail. Of course, there were plenty of other businesses as well. Like other boomtowns, Wichita had plenty of saloons, gambling dens, brothels, and dance halls where drovers could spend some of the money they had earned on their trips north.

Wichita was raucous and rough. In fact, its motto, quoted in Barra's *Inventing Wyatt Earp,* was posted prominently on signs along cattle routes that led to the town. It promised: "Everything goes in Wichita."

Because of its wide-open nature and annual influx of riotous cowboys, Wichita was perennially in need of lawmen. The drovers arriving in the fall were generally not criminals, but they were armed, lively, and—especially when drunk—often dangerous. Even a relatively innocent man who had no criminal tendencies could easily cause serious property damage or even endanger the lives of citizens.

On the other hand, the drovers provided welcome income for the town, so Wichita's businessmen were willing to tolerate them.

A Shy Young Man

Bill Dixon, who knew Wyatt Earp from their days as young men in the buffalo camps of the prairies, remembered his friend as smarter, more loyal and trustworthy, and more even-tempered than most of the men in that rough-and-tumble world. Dixon recalled:

> Wyatt was a shy young man with few intimates. With casual acquaintances he seldom spoke unless spoken to. When he did say anything it was to the point, without fear or favor, which wasn't relished by some; but that never bothered Wyatt.
>
> To those who knew him well he was a genial companion. He had the most even disposition I ever saw; I never knew him to lose his temper. He was more intelligent, better educated, and far better mannered than the majority of his associates, which probably did not help them to understand him.
>
> His reserve limited his friendships, but more than one stranger, down on his luck, has had firsthand evidence of Wyatt's generosity. I think his outstanding quality was the nicety with which he gauged the time and effort for every move. That, plus his absolute confidence in himself, gave him the edge over the run of men.

Maintaining the peace in a cow town was thus a delicate balancing act, which required enticing the drovers to stay while keeping them in order. In his book *Inventing Wyatt Earp*, Barra comments, "[L]ocal business interests expected the constabulary to keep the Texans under control, but could not afford to see them driven away."

It took a certain kind of man to make a good lawman in such a situation. When Earp arrived in Wichita, he seemed to be a natural fit for such a job. He was strong, smart, and solemn, sure of himself and not afraid of fights.

At first, he probably served as an unpaid volunteer marshal while earning enough money in other ways. In the spring of 1875, however, Wichita marshal Bill Smith offered Earp a paying job as one of his deputies.

There is evidence that the young man was also a part-time bouncer, hired to maintain order in some of the town's rougher bars. Earp's willingness to fight made him a natural choice for this job as well. Steven Lubet, in *Murder in Tombstone,* writes, "Wyatt's methods [were] always rough—he had no compunctions at all about head-banging for the sake of peace."

During his short time as a deputy marshal in Wichita, Earp began to mature. Up to then, he had been just another young man roaming the West and picking up work whenever he could. During this period, however, his character began to develop more fully, and he grew into what would become his familiar persona—one of strength, loyalty, and self-confidence, inspiring respect.

Charlie Hatton, a lawyer in Wichita when Earp lived there, later testified to this aspect of the lawman. Quoted in Barra's *Inventing Wyatt Earp: His Life and Many Legends*, Hatton stated, "I take great pleasure in saying that Wyatt S. Earp was one of the most efficient officers that Wichita ever had and I can safely testify that Mr. Earp is in every sense reliable and a trustworthy gentleman."

MEETING BAT MASTERSON

An 1875 article from the Wichita *Weekly Beacon* recounts how Deputy Marshal Earp found a drunken man passed out on the street with $500 in cash on him. The article notes that Earp did not take the man's money. Instead, he made sure that the fellow sobered up and then helped him to get home. The newspaper (quoted in Barra's *Inventing Wyatt Earp*) comments, "It is but justice to say he has made an excellent officer, and hitherto his conduct has been unexceptionable [without a stain]."

During his stay in Wichita, Earp met someone who would become a close friend. William "Bat" Masterson shared Earp's enthusiasm for and skill in gambling, a pursuit the two would enjoy off and on in the years to come. Masterson was, like Earp, a man of many talents and occupations. At times he was a peace officer, serving variously as a city deputy marshal, county deputy sheriff, and full sheriff. Masterson, who was also well known as a frontier scout, buffalo hunter, and, later, a newspaperman, would soon become an important figure in Earp's life.

During his time in Wichita, Earp distinguished himself as a peace officer in several ways, including the arrests of some horse thieves. But not all of Earp's experiences in Wichita were positive. According to legend, his loaded revolver once dropped out of its holster as Earp leaned back in a chair. The gun fired, and the bullet went through Earp's coat and into the ceiling. The lawman later denied that this embarrassing incident ever happened.

Earp's time as a paid Wichita marshal lasted just under a year. The job ended when Bill Smith, who had retired as Earp's boss, accused the deputy of abusing his authority to get his brothers hired on the force. (At the time, Smith was running against the current marshal, so he had a reason to paint the force in a bad light.)

Earp and Smith came to blows over the accusations, and Earp beat his former boss badly. In the wake of the incident, the younger man was fired and arrested for disturbing the peace. Although he did not serve a jail sentence for the offense, Earp was ready to move on. His welcome in Wichita, he clearly saw, was worn out.

Moreover, Earp liked to be where there was plenty of action, and he felt that Wichita was not the exciting town it once had been. The cattle trade was slowing down, and the place was becoming increasingly civilized.

So Earp moved on to another boomtown: Dodge City, Kansas. Dodge City was a former buffalo camp that, unlike Wichita, was rising fast as a major cow town. It was situated along the most famous of the routes the cattle drives took north: the Chisholm Trail, which ran from southern Texas to Abilene, Kansas.

DODGE CITY

Earp was not alone when he arrived in Dodge City. He had left Wichita with a companion, a former brothel worker named Celia Anne "Mattie" Blaylock. Although there's no record of their being

Dodge City, Kansas, had a reputation for corruption, with the city led by gang members and gunfighters. The Dodge City Peace Commission assisted with law enforcement and helped return the city to normal. Members of the Dodge City Peace Commission (*left to right*): Charles Bassett, W.H. Harris, Wyatt Earp, Luke Short, L. McLane, Bat Masterson, and Neal Brown, ca. 1883.

married, Mattie and Wyatt remained common-law husband and wife until 1882.

In 1876, when Earp arrived, Dodge City was only two years old as an official town, but it was already a hot and dusty collection of a few hundred people. Its streets were lined with wooden sidewalks, ramshackle wooden buildings with false fronts, and tents for businesses that had not yet moved into more permanent shelter.

Its noisy, dirty streets were filled with a variety of wagons, horses, and other means of travel. Drovers, cattle buyers, soldiers from nearby Fort Dodge, buffalo hunters, workers from the newly arrived railroad line, and others filled the streets. Surrounding the town proper were ranches and farms owned by a range of people, from the well-to-do to those who barely made a living from the dry soil.

Dodge City was growing quickly, as business in "The Queen of the Cow Towns" boomed, and that inevitably led to various illegal enterprises. Tefertiller, in *Wyatt Earp: The Life Behind the Legend*, quotes a reporter from Atchison, Kansas, who commented that the town was "infested principally with gamblers, horse thieves, prostitutes and murderers, who look upon the law as a huge joke." The soaring rates of murder, public drunkenness, and other crimes naturally created a need for tough cops.

Luckily, the trouble Earp had gotten into in Wichita did not get in his way and he was able to find work as a lawman in Dodge City. He was soon hired as a deputy marshal. (He was never the marshal there, as he claimed in later years.) Barra comments in *Inventing Wyatt Earp*, "Wyatt was no legend when he rode into Dodge on May 19, but he was not unknown in the territory. He was immediately hired by the Dodge City police force under Marshal Larry Deger, an indication [of] Wyatt's reputation as a good, tough cop."

Swank Barrooms, Stray Dogs, and Broken Sidewalks

Dodge did have some elegant aspects to counteract its seamy side. For instance, the town had a number of handsome, spacious saloons that generally served a "free lunch"—a complimentary array of snacks, offered all day. Barra comments in his book that these establishments

> served cold lager [beer] twenty-four hours a day, and from late morning till midnight a passing cowhand was free to partake of lunch, which included pickles and several types of cheeses and sometimes even caviar....

At night, gaslights reflected off the polished wood to give the saloons a sepia glow, and music from pianos and banjos wafted along Front Street.

As in Wichita, Earp's duties as a deputy marshal were not always dangerous. When not actively "sheriffing," he was occupied with more mundane tasks around town. These included hauling away dead animals, keeping packs of wild dogs out of the streets, and repairing the town's wooden sidewalks. Barra continues, "Wyatt shot a great many more stray dogs suspected of carrying rabies than he did cowhands."

Earp thus had plenty of opportunities to pursue other ventures during the slow seasons, and he often rode out of Dodge to follow them. There is evidence, for instance, that he spent the winter of 1876–1877 in another famous boomtown, Deadwood. This settlement was growing up around a gold rush in what was then Dakota Territory. The next winter, Earp went on another extended journey, this time traveling to Texas to gamble.

Despite these frequent absences, Earp was apparently well regarded by the citizens of Dodge. According to an article in *The Dodge City Times*, "Wyatt Earp, the most efficient officer this town has ever known, has just returned from Texas. He was immediately reappointed Marshal by our city dads, much to their credit." On another occasion, in an article cited in Tefertiller's *Wyatt Earp: The Life Behind the Legend*, the paper stated,

> Wyatt Earp, who was on our police force last summer, is in town again. We hope that he will accept a position on the force once more. He had a quiet way of taking the most desperate characters into custody which invariably gave one the impression that the city was able to enforce or mandate and preserve her dignity. It wasn't considered policy to draw a gun on Wyatt unless you got the drop and meant to burn powder without any preliminary talk.

Dentist John Henry "Doc" Holliday (*above*) became a close friend of Wyatt Earp after Holliday saved Earp's life during an argument. Holliday was said to be as fast at drawing his gun as Wild Bill Hickok.

MEETING DOC HOLLIDAY

It was probably on this trip, in the town of Fort Griffin, Texas, that Earp met someone who would play an important role later in his life. This was a tall, slim dentist turned card player and gunman from Georgia. Physically, he was unimpressive; moreover, he was a serious alcoholic, and was consumptive (the term used then for someone with tuberculosis). These problems did not, however, make him any less formidable a gambler.

His name was John Henry Holliday, but he was better known as Doc Holliday. Many years later, Earp summed up his friend in a statement excerpted in writer Susan Ballard's article "Facts Any Good Doc Holliday Aficionado Should Know," on a Web site maintained by the historical magazine *Tombstone Times*. The lawman wrote of Holliday,

> He was a dentist whom necessity had made a gambler; a gambler whom disease had made a vagabond; a philosopher whom life had made a caustic wit; a long, lean, blond fellow nearly dead with consumption and at the same time the most skilful gambler and the nerviest, speediest, deadliest man with a six-gun that I ever knew.

The two immediately became friends. This friendship was cemented in the summer of 1878, when Holliday saved Earp's life. As the deputy sheriff was trying to break up a barroom brawl, a belligerent cowboy pointed a gun at his back. Holliday drew his own weapon and held it on the cowboy, forcing him to back off.

There are many other stories of Earp's gunplay from those days. On one occasion, a Texan, George Hoy, quarreled with the deputy. Hoy left but returned with friends. The group then fired at Earp and Bat Masterson's brother Jim as they stood in front of Dodge City's musical-variety hall.

The two men returned fire, and Hoy was badly wounded. He died a month later. It is not clear who shot Hoy, although Earp and Masterson each claimed that he had fired the fatal round.

If the shooter was Earp, it was the first time he had killed someone. The lawman was proud of the fact that he drew his gun only rarely, and he claimed that he had never killed anyone who did not deserve it. He preferred to rely on the force of his personality and, if necessary, "buffaloing" (the Old West term for hitting someone on the head with a gun).

Now entering his thirties, Earp had grown markedly different from his younger self, especially in his confidence—if only because he was convinced that his own moral code was strong and correct. Tefertiller comments, "The Wyatt Earp [of Dodge City] had matured markedly from the boy who found himself in trouble in Indian Territory. He had become a most self-assured man who stoutly believed in right and wrong—and in his ability to determine which was which."

This personal sense of right and wrong did not always work to Earp's advantage. Because of it, throughout his career as a lawman he remained unafraid to defy authority. On several occasions in Dodge City, for example, he threw city officials into jail because he suspected them of breaking the law.

Needless to say, such actions did not make him popular among some of the town's more prominent citizens. Similarly, a growing number of cowboys and others around Dodge City became enemies of the deputy. As a result, Earp had an increasing incentive to leave the town. He was ready to move on again, and resigned from his job in September of 1879.

GETTING OUT OF DODGE

Earp left Kansas altogether, intending to travel to New Mexico Territory. (New Mexico did not become a state until 1912.) He wanted to take advantage of the lucrative silver-mining boom in the region. Earp guessed, correctly, that mining camps were taking the place of cattle towns as the West's most active boomtowns.

Mattie Blaylock, along with Wyatt's brother Jim and Jim's wife, went with him. They brought along 15 horses to use in their plan to mine silver.

Their first stop was the boomtown of Las Vegas. (Originally called Los Vegas, this was not the town of the same name in Nevada.) Doc Holliday and his girlfriend, "Big Nose" Kate Horony, joined them there. "Big Nose" Kate was a colorful character. One story has it that she freed Doc from a Texas jail by starting a fire in a shed as a distraction, then held a six-shooter on the local marshal until he let Holliday go.

The group then traveled to Prescott, in Arizona Territory, where Virgil Earp was living. As in Las Vegas, their sojourn there did not last long, and the group was soon on the move again. This time, they were bound for another town where silver had been discovered. The town had the ominous name of Tombstone. It was probably named for a nearby silver mine, not for anything connected to the town cemetery. This cemetery, like many others in the Old West, was called Boot Hill because it was the final resting place of men who had "died with their boots on"—in others words, violently.

Virgil had been appointed a deputy U.S. marshal for the county and was well known and widely respected. In fact, Virgil had a much bigger reputation as a lawman than his younger brother Wyatt.

Wyatt liked his new home. It was lively, growing fast, and economically strong. According to Lubet's *Murder in Tombstone*, Earp later commented, "In 1879 Dodge City was beginning to lose much of the snap which had given it a charm to men of restless blood, and I decided to move to Tombstone, which was just building up a reputation."

Earp's experiences in the dusty streets of Tombstone would make him famous—in the Southwest and far beyond.

TOMBSTONE

Tombstone was a high-desert settlement at an elevation of some 4,500 feet (1,370 meters). Like many of Earp's previous homes, it was a wide-open town of hard-drinking, hard-living men (and a few women), and it had a reputation for frequent gunfights. Its cemetery was one of the largest in the Southwest, and many of the town's buildings were pocked with bullet holes. Marks, in *And Die in the West*, quotes the impression one traveler had: "Every house is a saloon and every other house is a gambling he--."

Adding to the town's "snap" was the danger posed by bands of hostile Apache Indians, as well as numerous livestock rustlers and bandits (many of them Mexican) who roamed the region. These dangerous people made travel to and from the settlement risky.

Despite the violence and danger, however, Tombstone was growing fast. So many people were arriving every day in hopes of striking it rich in the silver mines that the pace of construction could not keep up with the demand. When Earp arrived, the town had more temporary tents than permanent buildings.

FINDING WORK

At first, Wyatt and his party rented a small house with adobe walls and a dirt floor. They staked several silver-mining claims and began working them. Jim Earp also found work as a barkeeper.

The town of Tombstone, Arizona, was founded in 1879 after a prospector discovered a lode of silver ore in the hills east of the San Pedro River. Tombstone soon became a boomtown, with services that included ice refrigeration, running water, telegraph and limited telephone service, and a newspaper. In only three years, the town grew from a population of 1,000 to an estimated 5,000 to 15,000.

Wyatt had hoped to start a stagecoach service, but was forced to change his plans. There was a lot of competition in this line of work, and a couple of similar businesses had already been established. Earp later commented, as quoted in Tefertiller's *Wyatt Earp*, "When I got there I found there was two stage lines and so I finally sold my outfit to one of the [other] companies."

Earp then found work as a security man with Wells Fargo, one of the companies that specialized in transporting money and other valuables around the West. Earp's job was to carry a shotgun on company stagecoaches. (The usual practice was to sit next to the driver—thus, the origin of the phrase "riding shotgun," meaning sitting next to the driver of a car.)

Soon, more of Earp's family and friends arrived in town. In the summer of 1880, Morgan and Warren Earp settled there. Doc

The Laws in Tombstone

While the Earp brothers were among the upholders of the law in Tombstone, the town had a number of regulations limiting the carrying of guns within its borders. These were meant to force people stopping in town to give up their weapons until they left. The usual practice was to surrender the weapons at the first corral or hotel seen. The relevant portion of the Tombstone bylaws read:

Ordinance No. 9: To Provide against Carrying of Deadly Weapons (effective April 19, 1881)

Section 1: It is hereby declared to be unlawful for any person to carry deadly weapons, concealed or otherwise [except the same be carried openly in sight, and in the hand] within the limits of the City of Tombstone.

Section 2: This prohibition does not extend to persons immediately leaving or entering the city, who, with good faith, and within reasonable time are proceeding to deposit, or take from the place of deposit such deadly weapon.

Section 3: All fire-arms of every description, and bowie knives and dirks [long daggers with straight blades] are included within the prohibition of this ordinance.

Holliday, who had been drifting around the region, also arrived to join the group and try his luck in Tombstone.

After his stint with Wells Fargo, Wyatt became a lawman again, joining Virgil as a deputy U.S marshal for the region. The nearest federal marshal was based about 280 miles (450 km) away, so local representatives of the federal government were needed in sparsely populated areas like the one around Tombstone.

By most accounts, Earp was a competent and respected lawman in his latest home. A lawyer cited in Tefertiller's *Wyatt Earp* who lived in Tombstone later commented, "His conduct as a peace officer was above reproach. He was quiet, but absolutely fearless in the discharge of his duties. He usually went about in his shirtsleeves without a coat and with no weapon in sight. He was cool and never excited, but determined and courageous."

One of Earp's adventures during this period involved saving the life of a gambler named Mike O'Rourke, known as "Johnny behind the deuce." The gambler was in danger of being lynched by an angry mob after he was arrested for murdering a miner.

Johnny insisted he had killed the miner in self-defense. According to legend, Earp stood off a large crowd that was trying to lynch the gambler before he could be tried, thus risking his own life and defusing the situation without violence. As quoted by Tefertiller, the lawman commented later, "They could have gotten me easily, but no one fired a shot."

CURLY BILL

Another of Earp's experiences as a lawman in Tombstone occurred when the town's sheriff, Fred White, tried to break up a rowdy and drunken group of men one night. White was shot while trying to take away the pistol of one of these men, "Curly Bill" Brocius. Earp and his brother Morgan came to White's aid, accompanied by a Wells Fargo agent. Wyatt was able to hit Brocius over the head with a gun butt and disarm him. The lawman then arrested Brocius on an assault charge. White died of his wounds.

The next day, Wyatt and another deputy took Brocius to the larger town of Tucson to stand trial for murder. The judge there ruled that the shooting was accidental, and ordered that Brocius be set free. The incident made Curly Bill into a determined enemy of the Earps, and from that point on, the brothers had to be on constant guard against him.

Characteristically, Wyatt's time as a deputy U.S. marshal came to an early end. He resigned in November 1880 after serving only three months. The Earp boys were beginning to make money on their mining claims, and Wyatt wanted to spend more time on that project.

THE COWBOYS

Early in January 1881, Earp used some of his mining profits to go into business on his own. He became part owner of the gambling concession at the Oriental Saloon, one of the most elegant of Tombstone's many drinking and dancing halls. One of his duties there was to oversee a popular card game called faro.

Now a private citizen, Earp sometimes got caught up in violent situations. On one occasion, a rival gambling operator hired a man named John Tyler to make trouble at the Oriental. The idea was to disrupt Earp's business. Tyler deliberately lost a bet and used it as an excuse to become belligerent and start fighting. Earp threw him out of the saloon. After that, there was no more trouble from Tyler.

A serious problem Earp faced came from the sharply increasing tension between the Earp brothers and two other sets of brothers, the Clantons and the McLaurys, who were part of an informal gang that called itself the Cowboys. (The term was then often used loosely to describe the men who were not cattle drivers but who were at least occasionally involved in illegal activities.)

There were several reasons for the bitter rivalry between the sets of brothers. The Earps had charged the others with stealing mules from the U.S. Army and also had implicated them in an unsuccessful robbery near the town of Benson. During this botched crime, a stagecoach driver and a passenger were killed.

The Benson affair was just the beginning of the bad blood between the two groups. Virgil Earp, as cited in Tefertiller's *Wyatt Earp*, later commented, "From that time on our troubles commenced, and the Cowboys plotted to kill us. They . . . took an oath over blood . . . that they would kill us."

The sympathies of the residents of Tombstone were mixed. Not everyone hated the Cowboys or admired the Earps. For one thing, the Cowboys always had a lot of cash to spend and were good

In 1881, Wyatt Earp received a quarter interest in the gambling operation at the Oriental Saloon (*shown above*) in exchange for services as a manager and enforcer. While living in Tombstone, Earp became a controversial figure due to his involvement in political and personal disputes.

for Tombstone's businesses. Furthermore, both the Clanton and McLaury families were established and well-respected ranchers. Ike Clanton could be ill-tempered—he liked to drink and boast—but his younger brother Billy was popular, friendly, and hardworking.

Meanwhile, in the eyes of many, the Earp brothers were not especially trustworthy. Some of Tombstone's citizens regarded them as tyrants who were mostly concerned with guarding the town's business interests and abusing their power to further their own.

The Earp brothers thought they knew who was responsible for the Benson robbery—three desperadoes with ties to the Cowboys—but they had no hard evidence. Wyatt therefore instigated a secret plan. He told the Cowboys he wanted detailed information about the identities of the robbers, leading to either their capture or death. In exchange, he would give the Cowboys the reward money being offered by Wells Fargo.

Earp had his own reasons for making this offer. He was planning to stand for election as sheriff of Cochise County against the incumbent sheriff, Johnny Behan. Earp hoped that capturing the bandits would help him win the election. All three of the prime suspects, however, died in incidents that may have been related. Ike Clanton, the oldest of the Clanton brothers, was furious at this turn of events. He was convinced that Morgan Earp and Holliday were responsible for the suspects' deaths. Clanton accused Wyatt of telling both Morgan and Holliday about the secret deal.

There was an unusual angle to the case. Doc Holliday himself was, for a time, accused of being one of the three bandits. Holliday's accuser was none other than his companion, "Big Nose" Kate. Doc and Kate had quarreled during a heavy drinking bout, and she wanted revenge. Nonetheless, the accusation was baseless, and at the ensuing trial, Earp testified and helped Holliday clear his name.

TRACKING SPENCE AND STILWELL

While the Benson investigation was continuing, Wyatt and Virgil Earp took part in the sheriff's posse that rode out to track two desperados named Spence and Stilwell. These men were implicated in another robbery, that of a passenger stagecoach near the town of Bisbee.

While on the trail, Wyatt discovered the print of a boot heel. It was unusually wide and had been custom-repaired. In Bisbee, Earp checked with a shoe repair shop that was known to fix extra-wide heels. Its owners confirmed that Stilwell had been a recent customer. The posse then confronted Spence and Stilwell at a Bisbee corral. Stilwell's boots had a new set of custom-made wide heels that matched the prints Earp had found on the trail.

On the strength of this discovery, Spence and Stilwell were arrested and jailed. They were released on bail, but a month later Virgil Earp, a deputy U. S. marshal, arrested them again on a new charge: mail robbery near the mining town of Contention City. Robbing the mail was a federal offense and, at that time, considered far more serious than other kinds of robbery.

Wyatt and Virgil rode to Bisbee to testify in the mail-robbery hearing. Back in Tombstone, meanwhile, Frank McLaury confronted Morgan Earp. Frank told Morgan that the McLaurys would kill all of the Earp brothers if they tried to arrest Spence, Stilwell, or any of the McLaurys again. The situation was growing more and more volatile. By late October, a showdown seemed inevitable.

A DRUNKEN ARGUMENT

The weekend before the decisive confrontation, Doc Holliday was out of town, gambling in the town of Tucson, to the northwest. When it appeared that trouble with the Cowboys was very near, Morgan Earp rode to Tucson and alerted Holliday. The two returned to Tombstone, and Virgil Earp deputized both of them.

On October 25, Ike Clanton and Tom McLaury drove a wagon into Tombstone to buy supplies. That night, around midnight, Ike Clanton got into a verbal fight with Holliday and Morgan Earp in a cafe-bar. According to some accounts, Clanton threatened to kill Holliday and the Earps. Other accounts claim it was Holliday who threatened Clanton.

The Earp brothers were present and watched the drunken argument until Virgil stepped in and threatened to arrest both Holliday and Clanton if they continued. Wyatt and Virgil convinced Doc to go to his room in a boardinghouse called the Harwood House so he could sleep it off. Wyatt went home as well.

Meanwhile, Virgil made an effort to calm everyone else's nerves. He spent the night playing cards at the Occidental Saloon with Ike Clanton, Tom McLaury, Cochise County Sheriff Johnny Behan, and another, unidentified man. Ike Clanton later testified that Virgil Earp kept a pistol resting on his lap the whole night.

Around 6 or 7 A.M. on October 26, the card game broke up. Clanton was still drunk and making threats. According to Tefertiller's *Wyatt Earp*, Virgil later testified that he said, "Ike, I am an officer, and I don't want to hear you talking that way at all. I am going down home now, to go to bed, and I don't want you to raise any disturbance while I am in bed."

Unwilling to ride home or rent a room in town, McLaury and Clanton continued to drink heavily. Later that morning, Clanton retrieved his rifle and pistol from the West End Corral, where he had left his wagon. He had been required to do this; Tombstone prohibited anyone from carrying guns within the city limits except under special circumstances.

Clanton was thus not just drunk and spoiling for a fight—he was also breaking the law. Furthermore, he was continuing to say loudly that he was looking for Holliday and the Earps so that he could shoot them down. One of Virgil's deputies roused him and Morgan to report on Clanton's threats. Around noon, the Earp brothers confronted Clanton in the middle of Fourth Street, which ran perpendicular to Fremont Street, the town's main drag.

Virgil promptly buffaloed Ike. As quoted in *Wyatt Earp*, the marshal later recalled, "I asked him if he was hunting for me. He said he was, and if he had seen me a second sooner he would have killed me. I arrested Ike for carrying firearms, I believe was the charge, inside the city limits." Virgil then took Ike to the court of Judge Albert O. Wallace for detention, but the judge happened to be away, performing a wedding ceremony.

Virgil went off in search of the judge, leaving Ike and Ike's weapons in the care of his brother Morgan. When the lawman returned, he had the judge with him. Judge Wallace fined Ike $25, which Clanton reluctantly paid.

Frank and Billy Ride In

At about the same time, Wyatt confronted Tom McLaury. Earp hoped to force him to reveal a concealed pistol he believed McLaury had. When McLaury refused to show him his weapon, Wyatt buffaloed him, but McLaury still did not draw a weapon. It has never been proved that McLaury was indeed armed.

Shortly after these confrontations, two more Cowboys rode into town: Ike Clanton's teenage brother Billy and Tom McLaury's older brother Frank. They had come to support their brothers in case of trouble. Frank and Billy were both armed with pistols and rifles, and they did not follow the law and disarm themselves when they rode past the city limits.

It was generally understood, however, that travelers could pass through town while armed, if they were on their way directly to a hotel or saloon, and this is what Frank and Billy did. They did not leave their horses at a corral, but rode on to the Grand Hotel on Allen Street. There, they learned that the Earps had roughed up their brothers. Frank and Billy immediately left in search of their rivals.

Probably the first place Billy and Frank went was a gun and hardware store run by a man named George Spangenberg. They needed to buy ammunition. Ike Clanton was already there, along with a young friend of the Clantons named Billy Claiborne, and possibly Tom McLaury. Ike had been trying to buy a pistol, but Spangenberg refused to sell. According to Ike's later testimony, cited in Tefertiller's *Wyatt Earp*, "The gentleman who owns the gunshop remarked that my head was bleeding, that I had been in trouble and he would not let me have it. My physical condition was such that . . . I was sick and bleeding [from the head injury Virgil Earp had inflicted]."

As Billy and Frank entered the shop, Wyatt was smoking a cigar outside a nearby saloon. He was not officially a peace officer at this point and had no legal authority to question the Cowboys' weapons possession. In fact, he was unable to do anything more aggressive than move Frank McLaury's horse off the sidewalk when it strayed and poked its nose into the gunshop window.

Unlike his brother, Virgil Earp did have the right to detain or arrest the McLaurys and Clantons; however, he deliberately avoided going near the gun shop. He hoped to avoid a violent confrontation.

The Cowboys left the shop and headed toward one of the town's corrals, the O.K. Corral. When Virgil learned of this, he decided to disarm them only if they were still armed when they left the corral. This would have been an intentional violation of the law.

The Cowboys did not go as far as the O.K. Corral. Instead, most of them gathered in a vacant lot about a block north. The lot was on

Fremont Street, immediately west of a boarding house and photo gallery owned by Camillus "Buck" Fly. It was also about half a block east of the West End Corral. There has been speculation that the Cowboys intended to use the West End as a jumping-off point for leaving town.

A railroad engineer from out of town, H. F. Sills, happened to be nearby. Not being from Tombstone, he did not recognize the men. The engineer later testified that he overheard the group talking loudly. As reported in Tefertiller's *Wyatt Earp*, the engineer stated,

> I saw four or five men standing in front of the O.K. Corral. . . talking of some trouble they had with Virgil Earp, and they made threats at the time, that on meeting him they would kill him on sight. Some one of the party spoke up at the time and said they would kill the whole party of Earps when they met them.

Not knowing who the Earps were, the engineer asked around and learned that Virgil was a peace officer. He then ran to notify Virgil of these threats.

Meanwhile, Johnny Behan, the county sheriff, confronted Frank McLaury about a block east of the vacant lot. Behan was a friend of the Cowboys, and he later said he tried to talk McLaury into disarming. McLaury refused, insisting that the Earps would have to disarm first.

Meanwhile, Virgil decided that violence was inevitable and armed himself with his pistol and a shotgun. He wanted to avoid alarming the town by openly carrying the shotgun, so he gave it to Holliday to hide under his long overcoat. In exchange, Holliday handed Virgil his heavy walking stick. With Wyatt and Morgan, they walked west down the south side of Fremont Street, keeping out of sight of the Cowboys.

"Let Them Have It"

Tombstone resident Martha J. King was in Bauer's Butcher Shop as the Earp party passed. According to Lubet in *Murder in Tombstone*,

The Cowboys and the Earps (with Doc Holliday) came face to face in a vacant lot near the O.K. Corral. Depending on which side is believed, the Cowboys were in the lot waiting either to leave town peaceably or to shoot it out with their enemies. Pictured is a mock-up of the gunfight at the site where it occurred.

she later testified that she heard Morgan tell Holliday to "let them have it." According to King, Holliday grimly agreed.

As the lawmen moved west, they met Behan, who was coming up the street from his encounter with Frank McLaury. Later testimony differs on what happened next. The Earps stated that Behan told them he had disarmed the Cowboys. Behan, however, said he told the Earp party that he had only tried to disarm them. According to Lubet's *Murder in Tombstone*, he told the Earps, "I am the sheriff of the county, and I am not going to allow any trouble, if I can help it."

In any case, Virgil and his companions ignored Behan and continued cautiously along. They knew that the Clantons and McLaurys were probably armed. It was now about 3 P.M. The lawmen walked toward the alley between Fly's and the Harwood House next door. They could see Ike Clanton talking to Billy Claiborne in the middle of the vacant lot. Behind them were Tom and Frank McLaury, Billy Clanton, and horses belonging to Billy Clanton and Frank McLaury. Most of the men appeared to be armed, and rifles could be seen on the saddles of the horses.

As the Earp party reached the alley, all of the Cowboys came out to meet them. The two sides drew together, facing one another in two lines at close range. Frank McLaury and Billy Clanton were next to the Harwood House, while Tom McLaury and Ike Clanton stood in the middle of the alley. Opposite them, Morgan Earp faced Frank. Doc Holliday and Wyatt Earp were in the middle of the alley, with Virgil Earp on the other end of the lineup, opposite Ike Clanton. Billy Claiborne, who was apparently unarmed, ran away from what was about to become a brief but deadly fight.

THE GUNFIGHT AT THE O.K. CORRAL

For a short time, both sides stood looking at each other but not firing. According to one witness, the standoff ended when Holliday poked a pistol into Frank McLaury's belly, then took a couple of steps backward. Virgil Earp, still hoping to avoid violence, commanded the Cowboys to throw up their hands and told his own men to hold their fire.

Ike Clanton came close to Wyatt and, grabbing his arm, said he was unarmed. As cited in Tefertiller's *Wyatt Earp*, Wyatt told him to leave: "The fight has commenced. Go to fighting or get away." Ike, like Billy Claiborne, ran several blocks and escaped the battle.

MORGAN EARP IS HIT

Back at the standoff, shooting began. Who fired first is still debated. Wyatt Earp testified later that the first two shots came simultaneously, as he shot Frank McLaury in the abdomen and Billy Clanton shot at Wyatt but missed. It seems, however, that the first bullets were fired by Holliday and Morgan Earp.

As the gunfire continued, Billy Clanton drew his pistol and was hit in his right wrist. He shifted his pistol to his left hand and kept

After the smoke cleared, three of the Cowboys were dead, and Virgil and Morgan Earp and Doc Holliday were wounded. Wyatt was the only one left untouched, which raised his reputation as a supreme gunslinger.

firing. Tom and Frank McLaury took cover behind a horse. Then the Earps heard a gunshot behind them. The shooter was probably one of three men who had come on the scene: Johnny Behan, Ike Clanton, or another Cowboy, Will Allen. Some sources speculate that this sound came not from a gun but from a ricocheting bullet striking metal.

In any case, the shot drew the Earp party's attention momentarily. Morgan turned to fire behind him. Either Tom or Frank McLaury used the distraction to fire over the back of the horse they were hiding behind. The shot hit Morgan in the upper back, above his shoulder blades. Nevertheless, he was able to keep fighting.

As this was happening, Doc Holliday emptied his shotgun into Tom McLaury's chest. The injured man let his horse bolt as he staggered into Fremont Street and collapsed. Holliday immediately tossed aside the shotgun and drew his pistol, firing at Frank McLaury and Billy Clanton. Both were still fighting despite their wounds. One of them managed to shoot Virgil Earp in the calf. Meanwhile, Frank McLaury shot Holliday in the left hip. Holliday's holster deflected the bullet, so he was only grazed.

Frank crossed the street, near the corner of the Harwood House and fired twice more, but a bullet (fired either by Morgan Earp or Doc Holliday) struck him in the base of his skull. Meanwhile, Billy Clanton was shot in the chest, abdomen, and arm.

"Such Lightning-like Rapidity"

The gunfight lasted only about 30 seconds, ending so quickly that the citizens of the town barely had time to realize what was happening. Tefertiller quoted the testimony of one bystander, Clara Brown: "The inmates of every house in town were greatly startled by the sudden report of fire arms, about 3 P.M., discharged with such lightning-like rapidity that it could only be compared to the explosion of a bunch of firecrackers."

The battle's aftermath was grim and chaotic. Tom McLaury, wounded by Holliday's shotgun, was carried into the Harwood House and died. Billy Clanton was also brought into the boarding house and lived long enough to be seen by a doctor. After the physician injected the gunman with morphine, a painkiller, Billy spoke only a few words, saying he had been murdered.

"Buck" Fly, the owner of the Fly businesses, retrieved Frank's pistol from the street. It still held two rounds of bullets. The coroner, Dr. H.M. Mathews, later came into possession of it. The horses that Billy and Frank had ridden into town were caught a few hundred feet up the street. Both had rifles in their scabbards.

The Earp party had clearly come out in better shape than their opponents. Not one of them was killed. Holliday was only slightly wounded, Virgil was shot in the calf, and Morgan was shot in the back. Wyatt escaped injury. Three of the Cowboys lay dead in the street: Billy Clanton, Tom McLaury, and Frank McLaury. This lopsided outcome was remarkable considering that the shooters, on either side, lacked experience in gun fighting. Although Holliday was rumored to have killed several men, Wyatt had been involved in only one shooting before. It has been proved that only one member of the Earp group had previously taken part in any extensive gunfighting: Virgil, who had seen action during the Civil War. Only one of the Cowboys had ever been in a serious shootout—Billy Claiborne, who had killed a man in a gunfight and had perhaps been involved in other battles—and he had left before the fight.

Ironically, the three Cowboys who were killed had little or nothing to do with the friction that caused the conflict. They were simply there to support the other Cowboys.

TOMBSTONE'S RESIDENTS REACT TO THE GUNFIGHT

Some of Tombstone's residents were outraged at the outcome of the battle. They considered it the deliberate slaughter of three men and gathered for a show of support for the Cowboys and their families. It was an impressive sight. The day after the battle, the bodies of the McLaury brothers and Billy Clanton were paraded through the streets in ornate caskets. A brass band led a procession of more than 300 people, with an estimated 2,000 watching from the sidewalks. The funerals that followed were the largest ever seen in Tombstone.

Still, most of the town's citizens were sympathetic to the Earps and Holliday. The *Epitaph* newspaper, as noted in Lubet's *Murder in Tombstone,* editorialized, "The feeling among the best class of our citizens is that the Marshal was entirely justified in his efforts to disarm these men, and that being fired upon they had to defend themselves, which they did most bravely."

Two days after the shooting, an investigation was begun. The coroner's report shed no light on the incident, since it stated only that the three dead men had suffered fatal gunshot wounds. Canadian journalist Ian Hunter, in an article titled "Ian Hunter on Doc Holliday: The revenge of Wyatt Earp" in the *National Post* newspaper, quotes the *Tombstone Nugget's* wry observation about this

The Newspaper's Account

Naturally, the shootout at the O.K. Corral was major news in Tombstone. The local newspaper, the *Sentinel*, reported:

A sanguinary [bloody] shooting affray [fight] occurred on Fremont Street this afternoon. Four [C]owboys have been in town for a few days past, drinking heavily [and] making themselves generally obnoxious by their boisterous conduct. This morning City Marshal V.W. Earp arrested one for disorderly conduct [who] was fined $25, which he paid, and was disarmed. He left the Justice's Court swearing vengeance.

The Sheriff, Marshal Earp and his brother Morgan tried to induce the party to leave town, but they were thirsting for gore and refused to be pacified. About 3 P.M. the Earp brothers and J.H. Holliday met the [C]owboys who drew upon them at once, when a lively fire commenced from the [C]owboys against the three citizens.

About thirty shots were fired rapidly, and when the smoke of the battle cleared away it was found that Jim [Tom] and Frank McLowry [McLaury] were gasping in the agonies of death. Bill Clayton [Clanton] was mortally wounded and died shortly after.

Morgan Earp was wounded in the shoulder, it is thought seriously. V.W. Earp received a flesh wound in the calf of the leg and Holliday escaped unhurt, with several bullet holes in his clothes. The streets immediately filled with resolute citizens, many of them armed with rifles and pistols. There is great excitement but no further trouble is anticipated.

Ike Clayton [Clanton], one of the [C]owboys, escaped with a slight wound, and is now in jail. The Sheriff's posse are now under arms. Morgan Earp, after he was wounded and had fallen, struggled to his feet and continued the fight till he emptied his revolver. His wound is not thought to be serious. The citizens are determined to put down the riotous element at all hazard.

finding's obviousness: "We might otherwise have thought that they were struck by lightning or stung to death by hornets."

Contrary to the popular image of the wild Old West, deaths seldom went unnoticed or uninvestigated, even in towns like Tombstone. Most towns had regulations, officers with the power to enforce them, and judges to sentence the guilty. In *Murder in Tombstone*, Lubet notes, "Outlaws were apprehended, arrests were made, trials were held."

Lawmen were not immune to this process, and Ike Clanton promptly filed murder charges against Wyatt Earp and Doc Holliday. The two were arrested and brought before Justice of the Peace Wells Spicer. Bail was set at $10,000 apiece. Morgan and Virgil, who were both recovering from their wounds, were not charged.

Even by the lawless standards of the Old West, the shootout at the O.K. Corral was considered remarkable. That is demonstrated by an article about Earp in the *Tombstone Epitaph* that was published just after the gunfight. It was headlined "Yesterday's Tragedy: Three Men Hurled Into Eternity in the Duration of a Moment," and it went on to note, "Stormy as were the early days of Tombstone, nothing ever occurred equal to the event of yesterday."

Newspapers across America also took note of the spectacular gun battle. A typical reaction was that of the San Francisco *Exchange,* reprinted in Gary L. Roberts' book *Doc Holliday*:

> The people of Tombstone have reason to congratulate themselves that they have not only courageous Marshals but Marshals who are dead shots. That performance yesterday, wherein three [C]owboys were left dead on the field and one lodged in jail, is among the happiest events Tombstone has witnessed, and especially so as it was attended by so little injury to the law vindicators.

THE TRIAL BEGINS

A trial date was set, and legal help for the McLaury/Clanton group arrived in the form of another McLaury brother, William, a lawyer in Fort Worth, Texas. As trial preparations progressed, it seemed likely that William McLaury's defense strategy would be to isolate and blame Doc Holliday as the chief catalyst for the killings. The defense attorney's reasoning was that Holliday, the day before, had started the confrontation with Ike Clanton that had ignited the violence.

Furthermore, according to some observers, Holliday had shouted threats as the Earp party approached the Cowboys just before the shooting broke out. Moreover, Holliday's reputation as a gambler and, allegedly, a killer made him a questionable addition to a party of lawmen who claimed they were determined only to disarm the Cowboys, not engage them in a gunfight. In the end, though, William McLaury did not use Holliday's strategy, preferring to attack the credibility of all the defendants.

The first witness for the Earp group, the defendants in the case, was Wyatt. He detailed the Earps' previous troubles with the Clantons and McLaurys and stated he and his colleagues had planned to disarm the Cowboys. The deputy marshal's full testimony is reprinted on the Web site maintained by the University of Missouri at Kansas City law school. It reads, in part:

> I was tired of being threatened by Ike Clanton and his gang and believe from what he said to me and others, and from their movements that they intended to assassinate me the first chance they had, and I thought that if I had to fight for my life with them I had better make them face me in an open fight. . . . [I told Ike Clanton] 'You damned dirty cow thief. . . . I think I would be justified in shooting you down any place I should meet you, but if you are anxious to make a fight, I will go anywhere on earth to make a fight with you. . . !' He replied, 'I will see you after I get through here. I only want four feet of ground to fight on!'

Wyatt Earp's further testimony indicated that he drew his own pistol when he saw Billy Clanton and Frank McLaury draw theirs.

When Billy Clanton leveled his pistol at the lawman, Earp did not aim at the young man. He stated, as reprinted on the same law school site:

> I knew that Frank McLaury had the reputation of being a good shot and a dangerous man, and I aimed at Frank McLaury. The first two shots were fired by Billy Clanton and myself, he shooting at me, and I shooting at Frank McLaury. I don't know which was fired first. We fired almost together. The fight then became general.
>
> I never fired at Ike Clanton, even after the shooting commenced, because I thought he was unarmed. I believed then, and believe now, from the facts I have stated and the threats I have related and the other threats communicated to me by other persons as having been made by Tom McLaury, Frank McLaury, and Ike Clanton, that these men last named had formed a conspiracy to murder my brothers, Morgan and Virgil, Doc Holliday and myself.
>
> I believe I would have been legally and morally justified in shooting any of them on sight, but I did not do so, nor attempt to do so. I sought no advantage when I went as deputy marshal to help disarm them and arrest them. I went as a part of my duty and under the direction of my brother, the marshal; I did not intend to fight unless it became necessary in self-defense and in the performance of official duty. When Billy Clanton and Frank McLaury drew their pistols, I knew it was a fight for life, and I drew in defense of my own life and the lives of my brothers and Doc Holliday.

Eyewitnesses

When it was their turn, the surviving Cowboys testified that Tom McLaury had been unarmed. They stated as proof that no pistol had

Although the Cowboys were popular around town, many of the citizens of Tombstone spoke up for Wyatt Earp and his cohorts after the shootout near the O.K. Corral. Even the town's newspaper, the Tombstone *Epitaph*, blamed the Cowboys for the fatal gunfight. Pictured are notable citizens of Tombstone.

been found on the body. Furthermore, the barkeeper at the Capitol Saloon testified that Tom's usual pistol had been left in the bar at the time of the shooting. Wyatt Earp countered that he believed a friend of the Cowboys had secretly removed Tom's weapon in the chaotic aftermath of the fight. Earp continued to assert this for the rest of his life.

As the trial continued, two disinterested witnesses testified. One was dressmaker Addie Bourland, who saw the shootout from her room in Fly's Boarding House. Her most important testimony was that not one of the Cowboys had held his hands up in surrender. She also stated that Billy Clanton remained standing and shooting for the duration of the fight, indicating he was not shot in cold blood as some contended.

The other disinterested eyewitness was Judge J.H. Lucas of Cochise County. Lucas had seen the events from his office in the

Mining Exchange Building, about 200 feet (61 meters) away. He confirmed the accuracy of Addie Bourland's testimony. Meanwhile, several witnesses for the prosecution testified that Tom McLaury had been unarmed, that Billy Clanton had his hands in the air, and that the McLaurys were not generally troublemakers. They also stated that the Earps had bullied Ike Clanton and Tom McLaury before the showdown. Furthermore, Sheriff Behan blamed the Earp party because it had fired first.

At first, it seemed likely that the Earps and Holliday would be convicted. The prosecution had built an impressive case, and sympathy for the McLaury-Clanton group was growing in Tombstone and beyond. For example, the San Francisco *Examiner* reported (as quoted in Hunter's *National Post* article), "Public feeling, which at first was for the Earps and Holliday, seems to have taken a turn, and now nearly all the people of Tombstone condemn the murderers." But then Ike Clanton took the stand and severely hurt his case. Ike's testimony was confusing, contradictory, and often clearly wrong. Tefertiller, in *Wyatt Earp*, comments that "when Clanton walked off [the stand], the entire prosecution case had become suspect."

In the aftermath of this damaging testimony, public opinion became more evenly divided. Lubet, in *Murder in Tombstone*, quotes Tombstone resident Clara Brown's letter to a friend:

> You may meet one man, who will support the Earps and declare that no other course was possible to save their own lives, and the next man is just as likely to assert that there was no occasion whatever for bloodshed, and that this will be 'a warm place' [an uncomfortable town] for the Earps hereafter.

In Support of Wyatt Earp

As the trial continued, a number of citizens of Wichita wrote a letter to Judge Wells Spicer in Tombstone in support of Earp. Their statement (reprinted on the Web site "Wyatt Earp, the Early Years") reads:

> We, the undersigned citizens of Wichita are well ac-
> quainted with Wyatt S. Earp and were intimately ac-
> quainted with him while he was on the Police Force here
> ... We further certify that said Wyatt S. Earp was a good
> and efficient officer, and was well known for his honesty
> and integrity, that his character while here was of the
> best, and that no fault was ever found with him as an of-
> ficer or as a man.

Spicer was inclined to agree. On November 30, about a month after the shootout, the judge delivered his verdict. He rebuked Virgil and Morgan Earp for bringing Holliday and Wyatt Earp into the conflict, since neither was a peace officer. Spicer also acknowledged that if the two had not been included, Virgil and Morgan would surely not have survived. Judge Spicer also pointed out that the un-armed Ike Clanton had been allowed to flee without harm, which spoke in favor of the Earp party.

Spicer therefore ruled that the killings were done in self-de-fense, and he acquitted all four defendants. Many historians have since weighed in with their own opinions and analyses. One of these is Gary L. Roberts, who says the shootout was nothing more than a tragic blunder caused by miscommunication. In his book *Doc Holliday: The Life and the Legend,* Roberts asserts,

> Stripped of all the rationalizations, post-fight justifica-
> tions and prevarications [avoiding the truth], the most
> famous gunfight in the history of the Old West was a
> bloody miscalculation that neither side really wanted but
> that both sides believed the other side wanted ... The Fre-
> mont Street fiasco was a testament to the costs of bragga-
> docio [boasting], miscommunication and rumor.

MORE BLOODSHED

The gunfight and trial were over now, but the bloodshed was not. Rumors flew that the Cowboys were out for vengeance. Indeed, numerous death threats were made against the Earps, Holliday, and Judge Spicer. According to Lubet's *Murder in Tombstone*, Virgil Earp later commented, "When Morgan and I got well, reports came in daily that we would be assassinated at the first opportunity."

Late in December, that threatened violence erupted. While Virgil, still recovering, walked the streets of Tombstone, he was hit by a shotgun blast. The lawman survived, but his left arm and shoulder were so badly damaged that he lost the use of that arm. The U.S. marshal with jurisdiction over the area immediately appointed Wyatt Earp to take his wounded brother's place. He also gave Wyatt authority to hire more deputies. Wyatt then sold his gambling concession to concentrate on law enforcement.

Meanwhile, Ike Clanton disappeared. Soon after the shooting, Clanton's hat had been found where Virgil's attacker had hidden. On it were the initials I. K. (Not everyone in the Old West could spell.) The hat, however, did not provide enough evidence to arrest Clanton. In those days, before the science of forensics was developed, virtually the only way to convict a criminal was to catch him in the act. Nonetheless, the Earps were convinced they knew who the culprit was.

Late in January 1882, Wyatt and Doc Holliday led a posse that hunted and captured Ike Clanton, charging him with shooting Virgil. In the ensuing trial, however, Clanton was acquitted. This verdict was reached after seven witnesses swore that Clanton had been in nearby Charleston at the time of the shooting.

Ike Clanton again filed charges against the Earps. They were arrested pending trial but did not spend all their time in jail. Virgil, still recovering from his wound, remained at home. Meanwhile, Wyatt was allowed out periodically, mostly so he could lead posses to fend off raids by Mexican outlaws from across the border.

Morgan Is Killed

Despite the continuing threats, Morgan and Wyatt refused to go into hiding. Then, one evening in March, Morgan attended a show and afterward visited a pool hall with Wyatt. As the brothers played, gunmen fired through a glass door into the building. Wyatt narrowly missed being shot, but Morgan was hit in the lower back. The bullet passed clean through him and into the thigh of another man.

Virgil rushed to the pool hall from his home, and a doctor was notified. Morgan, who had been placed on a sofa in the pool hall, survived for nearly an hour after being shot. According to legend, just before he died, the injured man asked Wyatt a question: Who did this? Wyatt replied that he knew, and Morgan's last words urged his brothers to find the killers.

At the coroner's inquest after the shooting, it was ruled that the likely suspects were four Cowboys: Pete Spence, Frank Stilwell, Frederick Bode, and Florentino "Indian Charlie" Cruz. Stilwell, Bode, and Cruz were long gone, but Spence turned himself in, hoping to be jailed for protection from the Earps and their supporters.

In the aftermath of the shooting, Warren and Jim Earp came to Tombstone to help deal with the burial of Morgan's body. The family agreed to bury him near the family home in Colton, California. Morgan's wife was already there. She had left Tombstone some time before for protection.

Morgan's coffin was loaded onto a wagon and taken to the nearest train station, in Benson. Wyatt and Jim Earp, along with Doc Holliday, accompanied their late brother. They wanted to make sure the body reached the train station safely. They did not plan, however, to take it all the way to California themselves. They felt that dealing with the violent business in Tombstone was a much more urgent task.

Virgil and his wife, Allie, had hoped to go to California as well, but their trip had to be delayed. It would not have been safe for them to leave town with Morgan's body. Besides, Virgil had not fully recovered. When Virgil and Allie did leave, some time later, they were accompanied by Warren and Wyatt Earp, Doc Holliday, and two friends, "Turkey Creek Jack" Johnson and Sherman McMasters. Two wagons were needed for this large party. The men who left with Virgil and Allie planned to take the train from Benson to Tucson. After that, Virgil and Allie would continue by themselves.

AN AMBUSH GONE BAD

As the group left, Wyatt received word that four Cowboys—Ike Clanton, Frank Stilwell, Hank Swilling, and an unidentified man— were in Tucson watching the passenger trains. It was clear they intended to ambush the Earp party. Despite the threat, the group continued to Tucson. After dinner in town, Virgil and Allie re-boarded the train while the others stood guard. As the train pulled out, shots were heard. Witnesses later testified that they saw armed men running away.

Scouting the area, Wyatt saw Stilwell and Ike Clanton lying on a flatcar with shotguns. As Earp approached, the men tried to run. Stilwell stumbled and Earp shot him dead. Lubet's *Murder in Tombstone*, quotes the lawman's later testimony:

> He couldn't shoot when I came near him. He stood there helpless and trembling for his life. As I rushed upon him he put out his hands and clutched at my shotgun. I let go both barrels, and he tumbled down dead and mangled at my feet. I started for Clanton then, but he escaped behind a moving train of cars.

The next morning, Stilwell's body was found on the railroad tracks. It had shotgun wounds and three other types of bullet wounds, indicating that someone besides Wyatt also shot him— although no one else was ever formally accused of the shooting.

Ike Clanton, meanwhile, had escaped by running away as he had done during the O.K. Corral shooting, leading many historians to speculate about the extent of his bravery. In a later interview with a local newspaper, Clanton offered an excuse for his presence in town. He claimed he and Stilwell had been in Tucson on an unrelated matter.

According to him, the pair heard that the Earps were traveling by train to Tucson with the intention of killing Stilwell. For that reason, Clanton said, Stilwell had gone to the station. Few people believed him, however. They scoffed at the idea that Stilwell would have willingly put himself in danger. Meanwhile, Virgil and his wife were safely headed for California. The others in their party, riding back to Tombstone, did not know yet that they were wanted men. Warrants had already been issued in Tucson charging them with Stilwell's murder.

Authorities in Tucson sent a telegram to Sheriff Behan in Tombstone, notifying him of the arrest warrants. But the telegraph-office manager was a friend of the Earps, and he showed the message to Wyatt when his group arrived home. Furthermore, the telegraph man agreed to delay giving Behan the message until the Earp party could plan its next move. When Behan eventually got the message, he sent a messenger to tell Wyatt he wanted to see him. According to "The Earp Vendetta Ride," an article on the Web site Legends of America, the lawman replied, "Johnny, if you're not careful you'll see me once too often."

THE EARP VENDETTA RIDE

On March 20, before Behan could act, the Earp party (now including "Texas Jack" Vermillion) left town. Officially, this group, which included federal marshals, was riding out to arrest Morgan's and Virgil's attackers. In fact, they were simply out for bloody revenge. Their journey, which lasted three weeks, is known as the Earp Vendetta Ride.

Meanwhile, Behan organized another posse. He deputized about 20 men, all of them friends of the Cowboys. Then the group set out to track down the Earp posse. Behan's group did not succeed in finding the Earp party, but that did not prevent Behan from charging Cochise County a small fortune for expenses incurred during the hunt: $2,593.65, roughly $57,000 in today's money.

In 1885, four years after the gunfight, Wyatt Earp visited the ruins of the O.K. Corral. Earp had left Arizona Territory in 1882.

On March 22, the Earp party began its campaign of bloody vengeance in earnest. The men rode into a camp owned by Pete Spence high in the Dragoon Mountains. Spence was still in jail, but Florentino "Indian Charlie" Cruz was there. According to Wyatt, Cruz confessed to being the lookout for Morgan's killer. The posse then shot him dead.

Two days later, in Iron Springs, the Earps found a group that included Curly Bill Brocius. Wyatt confronted Curly Bill as the outlaw cooked dinner. Both fired shotguns, but Earp killed Brocius and escaped injury himself. Another Cowboy, Johnny Barnes, was also killed. Some historians suspect that Barnes was the gunman who had crippled Virgil Earp. Their mission of revenge finished, the Earp party spent another two weeks in the rugged country around Tombstone. When it became clear that Behan's posse would not catch them, they began to relax.

They also knew they could not return to Tombstone. Wyatt, for one, was convinced he could not get a fair trial for Stilwell's death. So he and his comrades rode away from Tombstone for good. Wyatt's companion, Mattie, who had remained in town during the ride, stayed there in hopes he would eventually return.

In April 1882 Wyatt Earp left Arizona Territory. He was bound for Colorado, by way of New Mexico Territory. The next phase in his life was beginning.

ON THE MOVE AGAIN

On the way to Colorado, the group stopped in Albuquerque, New Mexico. About this time, for reasons that are not clear, Wyatt Earp and Doc Holliday had a brief falling out. Holliday went on by himself to Denver, Colorado.

The Earp brothers stopped in the small town of Gunnison, Colorado, where Wyatt took over the faro concession in a saloon. The marshal of Gunnison, Judd Riley, recalled that he had a good impression of the young man. According to Oldwesthistory.net's "Wyatt Earp Historical Home Page," Riley stated, "Earp was a fine looking man, tall with drooping mustaches that curled at the ends. He was quiet in manner and never created a bit of trouble here, in fact, he told us boys on the police force we could call on him if we needed help at any time."

THE DODGE CITY WAR

Shortly after his arrival in Gunnison, Earp rode back to Dodge City. He had been asked to help a friend in what became known as the Dodge City War. This conflict started when the mayor and the other town fathers of Dodge City tried to run a saloonkeeper named Luke

Short out of business and out of town. Their tactics included threats of violence and a trumped-up mass arrest of Short's employees. The mayor's group was on the side of a rival saloon owner who wanted to get rid of the competition.

To help resolve the situation, Short appealed to his friend Bat Masterson for help, and he in turn contacted Earp. Short traveled to Kansas City to discuss the matter with Governor George Washington Glick. Meanwhile, Earp arrived in Dodge with several friends: Johnny Millsap, "Shotgun John" Collins, "Texas Jack" Vermillion, and Johnny Green. The group marched up Front Street into Short's saloon, where Constable "Prairie Dog" Dave Marrow swore the men in as deputies. But the threat of violence came to nothing. To forestall real trouble, the town council offered a compromise. The council would allow Short to return for 10 days to get his affairs in order.

Earp refused to compromise and was able to stall Short's hostile enemies. By the time the saloonkeeper returned to town, no one had been able to organize a large enough force to turn him away. Short's Long Branch Saloon reopened, and the Dodge City War—not a war at all—ended without a shot being fired.

MEETING JOSIE

Earp returned to Colorado and rejoined his brothers, but their stay there was short. By late 1882, they were broke. Their property and other assets back in Tombstone had been sold off to pay for taxes. Meanwhile, the chances for making a living in Gunnison seemed slim. Wyatt and Warren decided to head west to San Francisco, California, by train. Virgil and his wife were already in California where he was seeking medical help for his damaged arm.

In San Francisco, Wyatt encountered a woman he had met before: an actress named Josephine Sarah Marcus, known to her friends as Sadie or Josie. Josie had a colorful and unusual background. In 1867, at the age of six, Josie had moved with her immigrant German-Jewish parents from Brooklyn, New York, to San Francisco. The

Marcus family was devoutly religious, and young Josie was given a Jewish education and instruction in religious practice.

Her life was far from quiet and pious, however. As a teenager, Josie was influenced by the romance of San Francisco's gold-rush era, when plenty of money was flowing through the town and there were ample opportunities to visit theaters, music halls, and the like. In 1879, at the age of 18, the young woman developed a desire to join this world by becoming an actress.

Josie went to see the Pauline Markham Theater Company perform Gilbert and Sullivan's operetta *HMS Pinafore*. With a friend, Josie decided to run away with the Markham Company when it left town. The teenager traveled with the troupe for some time and eventually reached Tombstone. While performing there, she fell in love with Johnny Behan, the local sheriff. Behan began a relationship with her, during which time he introduced her to Earp.

Josie and Behan split up, and she returned to San Francisco to resume her career on the stage. There, she and Wyatt encountered each other again and struck up a romance. The two would remain constant companions for the next 46 years.

They never formally married, but considered themselves husband and wife. Josie even took Earp as her last name. (Earp's former sweetheart Mattie eventually realized he would not be returning to Tombstone. In 1888, she died after drinking a bottle of laudanum, a medication that contained opium.)

Josie accompanied Earp on his restless wanderings. His need for constant movement may have been bolstered by a desire to bury the memory of his Tombstone days. If so, he was unsuccessful—for better or worse, his reputation followed Wyatt and his companion everywhere. According to *Wyatt Earp: The Life Behind the Legend*, "Tombstone would never be left behind them."

The couple left San Francisco in 1883 and spent the next decade in various boomtowns. One of these was the gold-rush settlement of Eagle City, in Idaho Territory. Jim and Warren Earp eventually joined them there. In Eagle City, the group invested their savings in about a dozen mining claims, ran saloons and dance halls, and operated gambling concessions. As was often the case in instant

Wyatt Earp and Josie Marcus traveled across the western frontier. They opened up gambling halls and saloons and invested in mines in Colorado and Idaho. Above is a painting of a gulch mine in the American West around 1890.

boomtowns, construction lagged far behind the need for it. Many of the Earps' businesses were housed in nothing more than rough cabins or tents.

A Final Meeting

Doc Holliday was already suffering from consumption (now called tuberculosis) when he and Earp became friends. The last time they met, Holliday was seriously ill. The date was May 1885 and the place was the Windsor Hotel in Denver, Colorado, on one of Earp's frequent journeys to that region. (Holliday died in November 1887 at age 36.) Earp's common-law wife, Josie, later wrote this account of the old friends' emotional meeting:

> There coming toward us was Doc Holliday, a thinner, more delicate-appearing Doc Holliday than I had seen in Tombstone. I have never seen a man exhibit more pleasure at meeting a mere friend than Doc did. 'When I heard you were in Denver, Wyatt, I wanted to see you once more,' he said, 'for I can't last much longer. You can see that.'
>
> They chatted for a few minutes then he and Wyatt walked away, Doc on visibly unsteady legs. My husband was deeply affected by this parting from a man who, like an ailing child, had clung to him as though to derive strength from him. There were tears in Wyatt's eyes when at last they took leave of each other. Doc threw his arm across his shoulder.
>
> 'Goodbye old friend,' he said. 'It will be a long time before we meet again.' He turned and walked away as fast as his feeble legs would permit. Only a short time after this we heard that he had died.

For example, for a time Wyatt and Josie opened a dance hall in a round circus tent, 45 feet (13.7 meters) high and 50 feet (15.25 meters) in diameter. It was advertised as the largest dance hall in the region. The Earp brothers also purchased a tent that they converted into a drinking establishment called the White Elephant Saloon.

In short, the group took on whatever moneymaking ventures it could find. Tefertiller writes, "The Earps were boomers, following the next big strike, hoping their fortunes would come in a mining camp where selling whiskey, dealing cards, and dabbling in claims could yield big returns."

MOVING TO SAN DIEGO

While in Idaho Territory, Wyatt became a peace officer again. There is evidence that in 1884 he was a deputy sheriff for a short time for Kootenai County. In the spring of 1885, however, Earp moved, at least temporarily, to the other side of the law. In Embry Camp, Washington (the present-day town of Chewelah), he joined a band of claim jumpers. (Claim jumping was a crime in which people took over a mining claim that was already registered to someone else.) There is also evidence that Earp may have jumped a claim in Colville, Washington, to the north. He was never arrested for these acts.

With Josie, he continued to wander the West, spending time in a variety of places, including El Paso, Texas; Aspen, Colorado; and Denver, Colorado. They eventually settled—at least for a time—in San Diego, California. It is likely that they chose San Diego because Virgil and his wife, Allie, were living there. Virgil was then working as the director of the Silver Gate Athletic Club.

The couple arrived in San Diego at some point in 1886. The city directory for 1887 listed Wyatt Earp as living at 946 Third Avenue. This was in a somewhat run-down and dangerous waterfront neighborhood called the Stingaree. The area was home to many bars, gambling halls, and brothels.

As with the other towns Earp favored, San Diego was jumping with activity. Shortly before he and Josie arrived, it had been just a small, sleepy beach town near the Mexican border. But after railroad lines reached the town and the public discovered San Diego's excellent climate, the population exploded. A town of about 5,000 in 1885 had skyrocketed to 40,000 by 1887. Earp took advantage of this dramatic growth by investing in real estate and opening a variety of businesses. For example, he bought several prime properties, including four saloons and gambling halls. The best known of these was the Oyster Bar at 837 Fifth Avenue, with a notorious brothel called the Golden Poppy above it. The building that housed these businesses is still standing.

Earp had other business interests as well. He occasionally promoted and refereed boxing matches, something he had done for years. Earp had been a skillful boxer as a teenager, so he knew well how to serve as a referee.

He also owned several racehorses. Over the next decade, Wyatt and Josie frequently traveled up and down the Pacific Coast, following the western race circuit.

A BOXING SCANDAL

After a short time, the couple returned to San Francisco and used it as a base. San Diego was experiencing a depression after the boom years, and the business climate was suffering.

In San Francisco, however, there were ample business opportunities, and Earp flourished. He often said that San Francisco was his favorite city, the place where he spent his happiest years. He and Josie had plenty of money—enough to luxuriate in fine clothes, expensive drink, and the company of wealthy friends.

Still, their time in San Francisco was not without problems. Perhaps the most serious was the result of one of the boxing matches that Earp periodically refereed. This was a title fight in December 1896 between two of the best heavyweights in the world: an Irishman, Tom "Sailor" Sharkey, and an Australian, Bob "Ruby" Fitzsimmons. Although boxing was illegal in San Francisco at the time, it was popular and openly tolerated by the police.

Earp thought that officiating at such a prestigious match might raise his standing in the public eye. Historian Barra, in a *New York Times* article titled "BACKTALK: When Referee Wyatt Earp Laid Down the Law," quotes the former lawman: "I don't know but what it will be a little bit of tone for me to referee a fight of this kind." But Earp's plan backfired when the incident became a scandal that made newspaper headlines around the country.

The first problem occurred when Earp removed his coat in the ring. He was wearing his pistol, contrary to local laws, and a

After a high-profile bout with heavyweight Bob Fitzsimmons, boxer Tom Sharkey (*above*) claimed the title of heavyweight champion. Wyatt Earp had served as the referee for the match and, in a controversial decision, disqualified Fitzsimmons for a low blow against Sharkey.

police captain in the audience noticed. Earp later said he had been wearing the weapon earlier in the day at the racetrack to protect against robbery and that he needed to be armed in case an enemy from his lawman days confronted him. Nonetheless, the gun was confiscated, and Earp was fined $50.00 for carrying a concealed weapon.

The next controversy erupted during the fight. Fitzsimmons, the favorite, threw a punch that knocked Sharkey down. Earp ruled that the punch was an illegal blow below the belt. He later commented in a remark reprinted in Tefertiller's *Wyatt Earp: The Life Behind the Legend*, "It was the most deliberate foul I ever saw struck." He then awarded the prize money to Sharkey.

The decision caused an uproar. Half the audience claimed they had seen a foul punch, and half said they did not. There were later allegations that the fight was fixed—that Sharkey had arranged the match to give the appearance that he had received an illegal blow so that he might benefit gamblers who had bet on him. (Earp may or may not have known of this arrangement, according to the allegations.) In the aftermath of the fight, Fitzsimmons sued Earp, but the affair was never clearly resolved. In any case, the lawsuit was thrown out of court—the judge could not issue a ruling about a fight that was technically illegal.

MORE TROUBLES

Although Earp was cleared of guilt in the affair, his reputation was badly tarnished. All over the city, and even beyond, the former lawman was the object of ridicule and insults. *Wyatt Earp: The Life Behind the Legend* comments, "Earp's reputation in San Francisco had been seriously damaged. . . . San Francisco had become, for him, a city filled with scorn."

The scandal was just one of Earp's misfortunes during this time. The former lawman was apparently still not above making the occasional shady deal. At one point, he was caught in a swindle scheme that would have taken $25,000 from a real estate agent. He gave the police a false name but was quickly identified. Since the scheme was not completed, the charge was reduced to a misdemeanor, a minor offense with only a small fine.

A more serious problem was that the real estate boom back in San Diego, where Earp still owned property, had completely collapsed in the spring of 1888. Houses were vacant all over town and unemployment had jumped. Burglaries increased, banks failed, and the town's population dropped sharply. As a result, many land speculators, including Earp, were forced to sell property to pay their debts. Gradually, Earp was able to sell most of his properties and other investments. Still, he did not escape financial injury altogether; he lost a great deal of money, and early in 1894 the San Diego *Union* reported he had been sued for nonpayment of a promissory note.

MOVING TO ALASKA

The time seemed ripe to move on again in search of riches. Wyatt and Josie left California in the fall of 1897. They planned to take advantage of yet another boom—a massive gold strike in what by now was one of America's last true frontiers: Alaska Territory.

The couple sailed north and spent time in several parts of this remote territory. One was the town of Wrangell, where Earp was apparently offered a job as a deputy U.S. marshal. He turned it down but volunteered to help out for a week or so until the town could find a permanent marshal. According to legend, during this period Earp met and made friends with the young Jack London, who later became famous as the author of *Call of the Wild, White Fang,* and many other adventure books set in the Far North. There is no hard evidence, however, to confirm this friendship. More certain is the knowledge that Earp was arrested several times during his Alaskan sojourn, for various minor offenses in different towns.

As always, Earp was keenly interested in making money. He and Josie put their energies into various plans to collect some of the abundant money that successful miners earned. One of his ventures was in Nome, which was then Alaska's biggest boomtown. Earp ran several saloons and gambling concessions, including the Dexter Saloon, the first wood building in Nome.

LEAVING ALASKA

Wyatt and Josie did not live in Alaska full-time. They traveled south to San Francisco or Seattle, Washington, during the winters that were so harsh the mines could not be worked and Alaska's population dropped. Earp may also have left once for another reason: in response to the fatal shooting of his youngest brother, Warren, in Wilcox, Arizona. The killer was a man named John Boyette, who disappeared soon after the killing and was never seen again.

Many people assumed that Wyatt and Virgil had traveled to Arizona and avenged their brother by killing Boyette. This, however, is unlikely. It took a long time to travel from Alaska to Arizona, and it is doubtful that Wyatt could have made the journey quickly enough. Meanwhile, Virgil was in California, but he was in very poor health and would probably have been unable to make the trip either. (Virgil Earp died in 1905 of pneumonia.)

According to some sources, Wyatt and Josie decided to leave Alaska for good when Josie became pregnant. She had already miscarried once, and this child would also die young. When the couple headed back south, late in 1899, they were flush with money. The Dexter had done well. When Earp sold his share in the tavern to his business partner, C.E. Hoxsie, Wyatt and Josie had more than enough to keep themselves living comfortably for several years.

The couple decided to settle for a time in Seattle, the biggest city in the new state of Washington. Like many towns on the West Coast, Seattle was wide open, awash in money that returning miners were bringing with them from the gold rush. The town was full of stores that sold equipment and supplies to men heading north to become miners. It also boasted plenty of saloons, dance halls, and other businesses designed to separate returning miners from their newly earned money. Of course, these latter establishments were of interest to Earp. In particular, there was gambling, which was technically illegal but tolerated in Seattle. When Earp arrived, one man, John Considine, controlled all of the gambling houses in town. Considine was happy to pay periodic fines to the city for operating his gambling houses. In return, Seattle's authorities allowed his establishments to remain open.

Naturally, Considine and his employees were anxious to stop anyone who tried to open up a gambling operation on their turf. Earp was used to such situations, however, and was not afraid of confrontation. He became the first serious threat to Considine's business. The former lawman did this by going into partnership with an established Seattle gambler, Thomas Urquhart. Together they opened the Union Club in what is now Seattle's Pioneer Square, then the main commercial neighborhood of the city.

The *Seattle Star* newspaper ran an item in November 1899 about the new gambling operation in town. Writer Pam Potter cites it in an article titled "Wyatt Earp in Seattle":

> SHERIFF FROM ARIZONA TO OPEN A GAMBLING HOUSE
> Considine's Combine Greatly Disturbed over the Outlook
> The New Man Refuses to Put Up
> Says He Will Run in Spite of Opposition
> Won't Knuckle to Chief of Police Reed or Anybody Else.

A MAN OF GREAT REPUTATION

Potter also quotes a notice in the *Star* the following month: "Earp and Urquhart's new house, the Union Club . . . is having a large patronage. When it was first opened, about two weeks ago, five games were run. Last night the management placed several new games on the floor."

Considine tried hard to intimidate Earp into closing. He threatened to have the chief of police shut the Union Club down, but Earp pointed out that the police would then have to shut down Considine's operations as well. These houses employed about

1,000 men and brought the city hefty amounts of money in taxes and fines, so the city was not eager to see them shut.

Earp was allowed to remain in business, and he quickly established himself as one of Seattle's more prominent sportsmen. According to Potter, the *Star* reported that the former lawman was "a man of great reputation among the toughs and criminals, inasmuch as he formerly walked the streets of a rough frontier mining town with big pistols stuck in his belt, spurs on his boots and a devil-may-care expression upon his official face."

HEADING SOUTH

As usual, Wyatt and Josie did not stay long in Seattle. There was a crackdown on gambling in 1900, and in the spring or summer the couple quietly returned to San Francisco. Potter comments, "Wyatt Earp . . . entered the Seattle gambling fraternity with passion, fortitude and resilience, and he slid out with nary a whisper."

For the next two decades, Wyatt and Josie continued to travel constantly, mostly in California and Nevada. In Nevada, they ran a bar in Tonopah, a town known as "the Queen of the Silver Camps." In Los Angeles, Earp was arrested for running an illegal bunco operation. (Bunco is a dice game.) Earp gave the arresting officer a fake name, William Stapp, and in any case was later acquitted of the charge.

Much of the couple's time was spent working mining operations, sometimes in the company of Earp's brother Jim. One such venture was in the Sonoran Desert town of Vidal, California, near the Arizona border. In 1906, in the Whipple Mountains near Vidal, Earp staked claims in copper and gold mines. The nearby town of Earp, California, is named after him.

During their travels, Wyatt and Josie camped out or, if possible, stayed in hotels and rental cottages. It is not known how much money they made prospecting. However much it was, it was sorely needed. Most of the profit from the sale of the saloon in Nome had already gone to pay gambling debts and other expenses. By now the two were growing old and beginning to tire of the ceaseless travel. They decided to settle down for good in Hollywood, California. There, the retired lawman was able to spend his last years in peace— and began to trade on his legendary status.

THE FINAL YEARS

Earp's last years were relatively quiet. He remained well-known, but the glory days, the times when he had been a feared lawman, were long gone. When he was younger, Earp had been a significant part of the rip-roaring Old West. Now, as the country became more and more settled, he seemed increasingly out of date. Tefertiller comments in *Wyatt Earp*, "The Alaska money gradually dwindled and Wyatt S. Earp . . . could not find another boom. Earp had become an aging frontiersman when America ran out of frontier."

STILL FAMOUS

To live out his final years, Earp settled down in Hollywood in 1906. The former lawman continued to dabble in a variety of jobs. He was still physically strong, good with horses, and unafraid of hard work. Earp sometimes found employment working on construction crews or driving wagons. Evidence suggests that Earp also was hired periodically to conduct secret and sometimes illegal missions for the Los Angeles Police Department. These apparently included chasing criminals who had escaped across the Mexican border. For a time, Earp also served as a deputy sheriff for San Bernardino County; however, this was mostly a ceremonial position.

When he was not working or gambling, Earp spent much of his time enjoying his public image. He relished being in the company of

In his final days, Wyatt Earp and Josie Marcus settled in Hollywood, California. He met several famous and soon-to-be-famous movie actors who were interested in Earp's story. Many would base their cowboy roles on their conversations with Earp.

people who knew about his past and admired his exploits. He was free to tell stories about himself, downplaying the negative while emphasizing the positive. There was little chance he could be called a liar since most of his old friends and enemies, including Doc Holliday and Virgil Earp, were now dead.

Earp's stories included his claim that he had faced down the notorious gunman Clay Allison, in Dodge City in 1878. Also Earp repeatedly said he was the one who had killed Johnny Ringo during the "vendetta ride" of 1882. Furthermore, Earp told a writer that he had arrested another gunslinger, Ben Thompson, in Kansas in 1873. No proof exists for any of these claims, and he may have made them up.

Another probably heavily exaggerated story concerns a gun known as the Buntline Special. According to legend, in his lawman days Earp often used this special Colt revolver, which had an extra-long, 12-inch (30-centimeter) barrel. The tale of the Buntline Special began with the death of a well-known actress, Dora Hand, in Dodge City in 1878. Hand was shot during an attempt to assassinate the town's mayor, James H. Kelly. Hand's death was sensational news and led to a manhunt for the killer, James Kenedy. Wyatt Earp was one of five key posse members in the hunt. Another was Bat Masterson. According to legend, Kenedy's capture inspired Ned Buntline, an author of dime novels, to present five custom-made guns—called Buntline Specials—to the posse. Allegedly, Buntline had specially commissioned this gun from Colt.

The guns did exist. In fact, Colt continued to make Buntline Specials for years in small numbers. However, there is no definite proof that Earp favored the gun or used it extensively, as he later claimed.

THE SILVER SCREEN

During his later years, Earp loved to visit the silent-movie sets springing up around Hollywood. In turn, the growing film community there welcomed Earp. Several of his former comrades from the Old West were working as stunt men, and Earp was sometimes hired as an adviser on cowboy movies. He even appeared as an extra in a 1916 film, *The Half-Breed*, which starred Douglas Fairbanks.

While spending time on movie sets, Earp met a number of famous and soon-to-be-famous actors. Among them was a young extra and prop man named Marion Robert Morrison. The young man hoped to break into acting, but fame eluded him until he took a new name. As John Wayne he went on to become the most famous cowboy actor in history. Wayne later said that he based his screen persona—that of a tough, honorable, reserved, and fearless lawman—on the stories Wyatt Earp had told him.

Earp also became close friends with two other Hollywood notables, William S. Hart and Tom Mix. Although largely forgotten now, Hart and Mix were the biggest cowboy-movie stars of their time. Journalist David Ashford, in an article titled "First Action Hero" in the British newspaper *The Independent*, comments, "These two Hollywood cowboys . . . were both great admirers of Earp, enjoying his company and proud to call themselves his friends. After all, he was the Real Thing—he had worn a lawman's star and actually shot down real bad guys."

Earp and Hart exchanged many letters over the years, even when they were in the same city (not uncommon at the time). This one, for instance, is from an article by writer Tom Murray on the Santa Clarita Valley Historical Society's Web site:

Oct. 21, 1920

My Dear Hart:
    I am sending you the quirt [a short riding whip] that I promised you some time ago and I am also adding a word of apology for the delay. My time has been so occupied with business affairs during recent weeks requiring my absence. I just did not get the opportunity to mail the quirt to you. Although I have thought of you.
    I believed I explained to you the quirt was made a number of years back in 1885 by a Mexican woman who

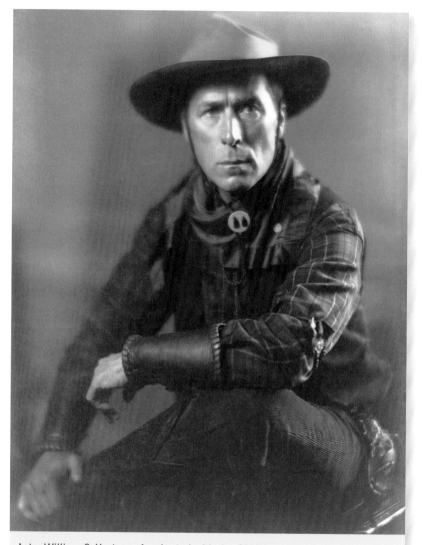

Actor William S. Hart was fascinated with the Old West and became one of the first great stars of film Westerns. Hart's great friendship and his conversations with Wyatt Earp and the use of authentic costumes and props served to make his western films more realistic.

was serving time in the penitentiary at Yuma, Arizona for the murder of her husband so you can see that a good quirt was made by a bad woman. It ought to stand hard usage and last a lifetime and I am sure it will. In your leisure moments may you occasionally remember that this is just a token of appreciation from me who hold[s] you in deepest regards and esteem.

Your friend,

Wyatt S. Earp

4021 Pasadena Ave.

Los Angeles, Calif.

POLISHING THE REPUTATION

During this period, Earp was also a regular visitor to the beachside town of Coronado, a popular site for vacationers. Many people set up tents and camped on the beach if they couldn't afford rooms in such nearby hotels as the lavish Hotel del Coronado.

Earp was in the habit of walking up and down the beach, playing cards with anyone who was interested. According to legend, he occasionally used his still-powerful physical strength and stern personality to settle public disputes and fights. But playing cards and other diversions did not occupy all of Earp's energies in his last years. A good deal of his time was spent giving interviews to newspaper writers, once again telling the stories about his past exploits to eager audiences.

A number of books about Earp appeared that significantly boosted the legend. Before this time, Earp had been only moderately well-known, mostly in the Southwest. Now he was well on his way to becoming a national figure. One of the first writers to boost Earp's reputation was an author of popular Western history, Frederick Bechdolt, whose book, *When the West Was Young,* was published in 1922. It painted a highly flattering picture of Earp. Another book along the same lines was Walter Noble Burns's *Tombstone, An Iliad of the Southwest,* published in 1927.

Earp was reluctant to help others tell his story, and he did not cooperate in the writing of either book, with the exception of one interview he granted Burns—under false pretenses. Burns told Earp he was writing a book about Doc Holliday. When the book was published and the real reason for the interview became clear, Earp was furious.

The book angered him for other reasons. For one thing, it related a number of completely false stories. Worse, Earp received no money from the book's sales. Its writer profited from telling the lawman's story, while the book's subject was frequently experiencing financial difficulties and even poverty. Tefertiller's *Wyatt Earp* quotes a relative of Virgil Earp's widow: "It was a bitter pill for him, and it made him a bitter man."

HELLDORADO

Helldorado: Bringing Law to the Mesquite, published in 1928 by Billy Breakenridge, was yet another dubious book. Breakenridge was a former deputy in Cochise County, Arizona, who had known Earp—but he was no friend. Breakenridge painted himself in a positive light and told a number of lies about Earp. In their 2008 article "The Making of Wyatt Earp's Legend" in *Wild West* magazine, Eric Weider and John Rose reprint a letter Earp wrote to a friend. In it, he wryly commented on Breakenridge's version of the shootout at the O.K. Corral: "Mr. Breckenridge tells that the Clantons and the McLaureys [sic] were unarmed and that they threw up their hands. All of which is very interesting, and probably explains how Virgil Earp, Morgan Earp, and Doc Holliday were wounded during the fight." The lack of truth in *Helldorado*—and the negative picture it painted of Earp—probably did more than anything else to convince Earp that he needed to tell his own story. With or without him, he realized, his life was going to be told, and he was tired of the untrue stories. He decided it was time to write his memoirs.

Earp had actually started work on an autobiography years earlier. In the early 1900s, he made his first effort to turn out a manuscript. He collaborated with a friend, John Flood; however, the book was poorly written and never found a publisher. Meanwhile, Earp's friend William S. Hart, the movie star, was interested in making a movie about the former lawman, and he was

The Belle of the Honkytonks

Josie Marcus was very concerned about how Earp would be remembered by the public. Her letter to actor William S. Hart, dated March 24, 1922, reflects this. It also demonstrates that Josie and Wyatt considered themselves husband and wife, although there is no evidence they formally married.

Dear Mr. Hart:

I wish to thank you most sincerely [for] your very kind thoughts in contradicting the nasty and ugly articles which appeared in the Sunday *Times* of March 12, 1922 regarding my husband. Mr. Earp only yesterday did learn of the unpleasant affair. I have called on the *Times* staff and have made it very plain to them that every untruth must be corrected and printed in the same sensational manner. I feel deeply indebted to you for your kindness to us. It was a mighty big thought of yours and we highly appreciate it.

I am leaving for the mines today where my husband is at present and [will] fully acquaint him of all this unpleasant affair and also tell him your genuine kindness to him. Accept our heartiest congratulations and wishing you and your wife every happiness in the world of which you are more than worthy. I wish to thank you once more for all you have done.

Very sincerely,

Mr. and Mrs. Earp

Near the end of his life, Earp and writer Stuart Lake planned to collaborate on Earp's autobiography. The former lawman saw the project as a chance to set the record straight; however, Lake and Josie Earp disagreed from the beginning about how the book should be written. At one point, a frustrated Lake wrote to his editor at Houghton Mifflin:

(continues)

(continued)

> Bat Masterson, and a score of old-timers, have told me that she [Josie] was the belle of the honkytonks, the prettiest dame in three hundred or so of her kind....
>
> Sadie [Earp's nickname for her] has proceeded on the theory that all I know is what she has chosen to tell me, has tried to cover up with a tissue of lies and deceptions which has been so transparent as to be pathetic. I have not chosen to disillusion her about her success.
>
> She dreads beyond my power to describe the chance that I may stumble on to the truth, fears that I may know it now, but lacks the courage to out with it and ask me to tell her what I do know.... She is the key to the whole yarn of Tombstone. Should I or should I not leave that key unturned?

After Earp's death, Lake had to deal with Josie on his own. The day after the lawman's funeral, he wrote to her,

> I do want to assure you, however, that the work of the biography will go on, to as speedy a conclusion as is compatible with accuracy . . . and the proper quality of the work.... More than ever, now, I also want you to place your confidence in my desire to do whatever is best with the story of Mr. Earp's life. . . . nothing can or will be done of course, without your sanction.

When the book was published, it painted the glowing portrait of Earp that Josie had been determined to create.

sympathetic when Earp's manuscript was repeatedly rejected. As Tefertiller notes in *Wyatt Earp*, Hart wrote to his friend, "I cannot figure what the devil is the matter with them. It may be some literary defect that they can see which is beyond our vision. However I am for hammering them until the hot place freezes over."

Josie also did as much as she could to help the movie plan along. Her efforts included making sure that Hart remained enthusiastic.

One example is a letter she wrote to the movie star in 1923 concerning a film about another famous figure of the Old West:

> My dear Mr. Hart:
> Just a line to congratulate you upon your new picture "Wild Bill Hickok." I saw it twice with several friends and each time the house was packed. When you appeared upon the screen the applause was wonderful. Am happy to say that you have staged a remarkable "come back."
> Trusting your future pictures will be as successful as your first.
> With kindest regards,
> I am sincerely yours,
> Mrs. Wyatt Earp

Earp's project to write a book was resumed in 1927, when he was approached by Stuart Lake, a newspaperman. A trusted friend, Bat Masterson, had recommended Lake to Earp. At the time, Lake and Masterson were both working at the same newspaper, the New York *Morning Telegraph*. A recommendation from this source was, for Earp, high praise. In a letter to Lake, quoted in the *Wild West* article by Weider and Rose, the former lawman wrote, "I am particularly interested in what you say about Bat Masterson. He and I were very staunch friends; a finer man never lived."

Earp and Lake hit it off, and they agreed to a partnership. They started their project in the summer of 1928. At first the former lawman had reservations: He was not in good health and worried he was not strong enough to complete the task.

"HORSE-HIGH, BULL-STRONG, AND HOG-TIGHT"

Earp commented on his poor health in a letter to Lake, saying he could not immediately judge his ability to collaborate. He noted that for several months he had been confined to bed and was just beginning to get confidently on his feet again. He planned to travel away from Los Angeles into the country, in the hopes of building up his health.

In time, Earp recuperated, and the two began their project in earnest. They usually met in the bungalow on West Seventeenth Street in Los Angeles where Wyatt and Josie were living. Always protective of Wyatt, Josie took an active part in the work and was especially concerned with the financial arrangements.

A letter from Lake to the former lawman makes it clear that Josie was also determined to control the content of the book. In their article in *Wild West*, Weider and Rose quote from this letter: "I hope that Mrs. Earp has been to her attorney and has become reassured about the business end of the collaboration. . . . To my mind, the agreement I offered was horse-high, bull-strong, and hog-tight with each of us getting an even break. . . . I wish that Mrs. Earp could come to feel that way."

THE DEATH OF WYATT EARP

The former lawman, who had been in poor health for some years, was seriously ill by this point. He did not live to see the manuscript of his autobiography finished. Earp died at home on January 13, 1929. He was 80 years old. The exact cause of death has never been determined, but it was probably either chronic cystitis (a prostate problem) or prostate cancer. According to legend, his last words were "Suppose, suppose." Josie leaned over to ask Earp what he meant, but he died before he could explain.

The lawman's death was major news, both locally and nationally. Many obituaries appeared, from small-town papers to large ones like *The New York Times*. Not surprisingly, they stressed his fame as a fearless lawman.

At the funeral, Earp's friends William S. Hart and Tom Mix were among the pallbearers. Josie did not attend, saying she was too grief-stricken. Earp's body was cremated, and the remains were buried in Josie's family plot at the Hills of Eternity, a Jewish cemetery in Colma, California.

WYATT EARP: FRONTIER MARSHAL

In the months after Wyatt's death, Josie was in difficult financial straits. Earp had left her with little, since he had always preferred to spend money rather than save it. Furthermore, he had never had much money in his last years. Tefertiller notes in *Wyatt Earp*, "Earp's final decade was one of . . . quiet poverty. . . . There were no Social Security payments or pensions for retired gamblers/lawmen."

So Josie repeatedly urged Lake to quickly finish the book, which she hoped would sell well. In the fall of 1929, the writer secured a publishing contract for the project. In their article in *Wild West*, Weider and Rose quote a letter from Lake to Josie: "If you leave it to me, you'll get a life story of Mr. Earp that will establish him in his rightful place. And that will make a little money for you at the same time." The process was not smooth, however. Josie remained fiercely protective of Earp's reputation, and she pestered Lake incessantly to make sure that the writer cast Earp in a positive light. When she finally saw a manuscript of Lake's draft, she still objected to several passages. By the time *Wyatt Earp: Frontier Marshal* was published in 1931, the offending passages had been removed.

The work was first serialized in a popular magazine, *The Saturday Evening Post*, and then appeared as a book. It was an immediate best seller. With money and many positive reviews coming in, Josie felt little need to complain. An uncredited article on the American Jewish Historical Society's Web site, "How Wyatt Earp Got Buried in a Jewish Cemetery," cites a December 1931 letter from her to Lake: "It is very gratifying to see so many favorable comments concerning both Wyatt and the manner in which the story of his life has been presented."

MAKING AND QUESTIONING A LEGEND

Wyatt Earp: Frontier Marshal played a vital role in transforming Wyatt Earp into a genuine American hero. In Lake's hands, Earp was a larger-than-life hero who was unafraid to use his six-shooter to ensure law and order. Tefertiller writes, "*Frontier Marshal* emerged as the story of a white knight on horseback, defending the populace against corrupt officials and vile desperadoes. Lake erased the many shades of gray from Tombstone to create a conflict of good versus evil, rather than exploring the complex questions that actually existed."

Thanks to the book, Earp's legend was born. As noted by the Ford County (Kansas) Historical Society, Lake asserted, "In true perspective, he is recognized as [symbolic] of a powerful factor . . . in the history of the Western United States of America. The Old West cannot be understood unless Wyatt Earp also is understood." Still, over the years, Earp's once-golden reputation has come under scrutiny. Many historians have questioned the authenticity of much of *Wyatt Earp: Frontier Marshal* and other books. They have looked into the evidence and have sought to paint a more rounded picture of their subject.

They point out the ample evidence about the less savory aspects of Earp's life, including his apparent dabbling in horse rustling. They also note the possibility that he may have been guilty of claim jumping, fixing fights he refereed, and perhaps other crimes. More serious are accusations that he aggressively misused his power as a lawman and helped initiate the O.K. Corral shootout. All his life, as historian Marks points out in *And Die in the West*, Earp walked "the thin line between law and lawlessness, respectability and notoriety."

EARPMANIA

Whether or not these accusations were true, it can be argued that Earp was only doing what was needed. Some historians point out that Earp lived in the rugged Wild West, where lawlessness and crime were rampant. Being a peace officer was a dangerous job, requiring a man who was brave and tough—and not afraid to bend the rules if necessary.

In any case, it is clear that there was much more to Earp than his work as a marshal. He devoted far more time during his life to prospecting, saloon-keeping, real-estate speculation, and other ventures than he did to upholding the law. In fact, Earp spent only about 6 of his 80 years as a lawman. Nonetheless, the popular legend persists that he was always honorable, brave, and charismatic. That image blossomed with Lake's early book and has since been nurtured in countless movies, TV shows, stage plays, and books. The influential book Lake wrote has fueled decades of Earpmania, in print, film, and other forms of media.

TRIBUTES

Although Earp's cowboy-star friend, William S. Hart, had always wanted to make a film about him, his project never appeared, though there have been many others. Among the most notable are *My Darling Clementine* (1946); *Tombstone* (1993); and *Wyatt Earp* (1994). Among the actors who have played Earp are Henry Fonda, Kurt Russell, Kevin Costner, Burt Lancaster, and a future president, Ronald Reagan. Furthermore, *The Life and Legend of Wyatt Earp* was a hugely popular television series of the 1950s. It starred Hugh O'Brien, who went on to appear as Earp in a number of feature movies.

Today, many towns associated with Earp honor the lawman with memorials. One of these is the small Wyatt Earp Birthplace Museum in Monmouth, Illinois. Another is the Wyatt Earp Room of the Gaslamp Museum in San Diego. And a statue of Earp and Doc Holliday stands at the train station in Tucson, Arizona.

THE LEGEND LIVES ON

A number of other locales also preserve the spirit of the exciting days of Earp's life and times. Among these is Tombstone, Arizona, which today attracts thousands of tourists annually with such Earp-related attractions as Big Nose Kate's Saloon, the Western Heritage Museum, and the Wyatt Earp House and Gallery.

Wyatt Earp was a legendary figure whose life became the subject of many films, books, and TV series. This scene depicts the gunfight at the O.K. Corral in the 1967 film *The Hour of the Gun* starring James Garner (*right*) as Earp.

Dodge City, Kansas, has created the Boot Hill Museum, and its Boot Hill Graveyard is also a popular attraction. Billy Clanton, Frank McLaury, and Tom McLaury, the three victims of the gunfight at the O.K. Corral, are buried in the Dodge City cemetery. (The Tombstone graveyard has the same name.) Meanwhile, Earp's own burial spot, in Colma, California, remains a popular draw for fans of the famous lawman. Visitors often leave poker chips, cards, bullets, and other tributes on his grave. Furthermore, Colma holds annual re-creations of the O.K. Corral shootout during a celebration called Wyatt Earp's Old West Days.

These tributes are just a few of the ways in which Earp's name is kept alive. For nearly a century, Wyatt Earp has dramatically symbolized the romance of the Old West. Despite the details that have gradually emerged about the less savory aspects of his life, Earp's place in the public eye—as the quintessential lawman of the Old West—remains secure. There is little doubt that this honor will continue well into the future.

CHRONOLOGY

1848   Wyatt Berry Stapp Earp is born in Monmouth, Illinois, on March 19.

1865   The Earp family moves to San Bernardino County, California.

TIMELINE

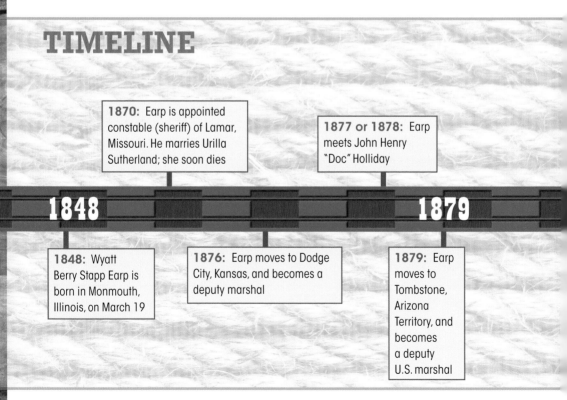

1870: Earp is appointed constable (sheriff) of Lamar, Missouri. He marries Urilla Sutherland; she soon dies

1877 or 1878: Earp meets John Henry "Doc" Holliday

1848

1879

1848: Wyatt Berry Stapp Earp is born in Monmouth, Illinois, on March 19

1876: Earp moves to Dodge City, Kansas, and becomes a deputy marshal

1879: Earp moves to Tombstone, Arizona Territory, and becomes a deputy U.S. marshal

1870 Earp is appointed constable (sheriff) of Lamar, Missouri. He marries Urilla Sutherland; she soon dies.

1871 Earp leaves Lamar and wanders for several years.

1874 Earp moves to Wichita, Kansas.

1875 Earp is appointed deputy marshal.

1876 Earp moves to Dodge City, Kansas, with a companion, "Mattie" Blaylock, and becomes a deputy marshal there.

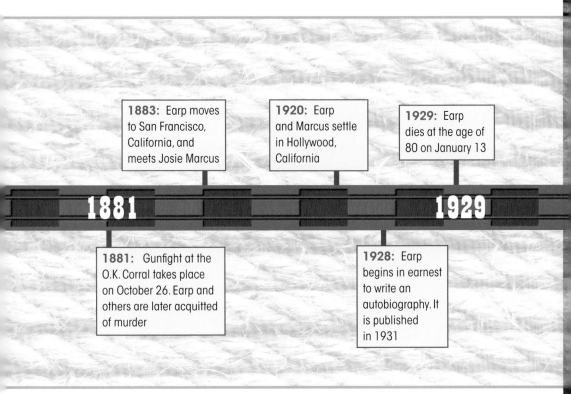

1883: Earp moves to San Francisco, California, and meets Josie Marcus

1920: Earp and Marcus settle in Hollywood, California

1929: Earp dies at the age of 80 on January 13

1881

1929

1881: Gunfight at the O.K. Corral takes place on October 26. Earp and others are later acquitted of murder

1928: Earp begins in earnest to write an autobiography. It is published in 1931

1877 or 1878	Earp meets John Henry "Doc" Holliday.
1879	Earp moves to Tombstone, Arizona Territory, and becomes a deputy U.S. marshal.
1880–1881	Earp resigns as marshal and opens a gambling concession in Tombstone.
1881	Gunfight at the O.K. Corral (actually on a nearby lot) takes place on October 26. Earp and others are later acquitted of murder in the event.
1882	Earp moves to Gunnison, Colorado, leaving Mattie in Tombstone.
1883	Earp moves to San Francisco, California, and meets Josie Marcus.
1883–1920	Earp and Marcus travel extensively, trying different enterprises.
1920	Earp and Marcus settle in Hollywood, California.
1928	Earp begins in earnest to write an autobiography. It is published in 1931.
1929	Earp dies at the age of 80 on January 13.

GLOSSARY

adobe   A clay-like material for building, common in the American Southwest

boarding house   A hotel, usually for long-term residents and usually supplying communal meals

boomtown   A thriving town that grows up quickly around an event such as a destination for a cattle herd or a gold strike

buffaloing   An Old West slang term for hitting someone on the head with a gun

cooper   A barrel-maker

drover   Someone who took cattle from a ranch to a railroad head for transport. The term generally became interchangeable with "cowboy."

embezzlement   Illegally taking funds from an organization

faro   A card game, now unpopular, in which players bet against the dealer on which cards he will draw from a box

prostate   A gland near a man's bladder

rustling   Stealing cattle or horses

skip bond   To leave town after paying a bond in return for release from jail

swindle   To cheat or "con" someone

typhus   A serious and often fatal infectious disease

vendetta   A stretched-out series of violent acts made in revenge

BIBLIOGRAPHY

American Jewish Historical Society, "How Wyatt Earp Got Buried in a Jewish Cemetery." Available online at http://www.ajhs.org/publications/chapters/chapter.cfm?documentID=279.

Ashford, David, "First Action Hero." *The Independent* (U.K.), September 3, 1994.

Banks, Leo W., "Reconsidering a Legend." *Los Angeles Times*, November 13, 2005.

Barra, Allen, "BACKTALK: When Referee Wyatt Earp Laid Down the Law." *The New York Times,* November 26, 1995. Available online at http://www.nytimes.com/1995/11/26/sports/backtalk-when-referee-wyatt-earp-laid-down-the-law.html?sec=&spon=&pagewanted=1.

———, *Inventing Wyatt Earp: His Life and Many Legends.* New York: Carroll & Graf, 1998.

Hamill, Jasper, "Legend of Wyatt Earp Is Shot Down 80 Years After His Death." *Sunday Herald* (Scotland), January 11, 2009.

Hunter, Ian: "The Killing after the Killing." *National Post* (Canada), July 30, 2008.

———, "Ian Hunter on Doc Holliday: The Revenge of Wyatt Earp." *National Post* (Canada), July 30, 2008.

Jay, Roger, "The Peoria Bummer: Wyatt Earp's lost year," *Wild West*, August 2003.

Lubet, Steven, *Murder in Tombstone*. New Haven, Conn.: Yale University Press, 2004.

Marks, Paula Mitchell, *And Die in the West: The Story of the O.K. Corral Gunfight*. Norman.: University of Oklahoma Press, 1996.

Peterson, Richard H., "In San Diego, Wyatt Earp Was All Business —and Business Was Booming for a While." *Wild West*, October 2004.

Potter, Pam, "Wyatt Earp in Seattle," HistoryNet.org. Available online at http://www.historynet.com/wyatt-earp-in-seattle.htm.

Rathner, Janet Lubman and Weider, Eric, "The Making of Wyatt Earp's Legend." *Wild West*, April 2008.

Rathner, Janet Lubman, "Wyatt Earp and His Jewish Wife," *Moment* magazine, July/August 2008. Available online at http://www.momentmag.com/Exclusive/2008/2008-07/200807-History-Box.html.

Roberts, Gary L., *Doc Holliday: The Life and Legend*. New York: Wiley, 2007.

Tefertiller, Casey, *Wyatt Earp: The Life Behind the Legend*. New York: Wiley, 1997.

Weiser, Kathy, "The Earp Vendetta Ride," Legends of America. Available online at http://www.legendsofamerica.com/we-earpvendetta.html.

FURTHER RESOURCES

Bloom, Barbara Lee, *Nat Love*. New York: Chelsea House, 2010.

Boyer, Glenn G., ed., *Wyatt Earp's Tombstone Vendetta*. Thorndike, Maine: Hall, 1994.

Green, Carl R. and William R. Sanford, *Wyatt Earp*. Hillside, N.J.: Enslow, 2008.

Hasday, Judy L., *Davy Crockett*. New York: Chelsea House, 2010.

Koestler-Grack, Rachel A., *Annie Oakley*. New York: Chelsea House, 2010.

Landau, Elaine, *Wyatt Earp: Wild West Lawman*. Hillside, N.J.: Enslow, 2004.

Reis, Ronald A., *Sitting Bull*. New York: Chelsea House, 2010.

Staeger, Rob, *Wyatt Earp*. New York: Chelsea House, 2002.

Woog, Adam, *Jesse James*. New York: Chelsea House, 2010.

Web Sites

Wyatt Earp

http://www.spartacus.schoolnet.co.uk/WWearpW.htm

This is a site maintained by Spartacus International, a British publisher of educational books. It includes a good short biography of Earp.

Wyatt Earp Museum

http://www.wyattearpmuseum.com/index.html

This is the Web site of a museum in San Diego, California, that is dedicated to the lawman. The museum has temporarily closed, but this site is still available. It includes photos of details of the museum's many displays.

Wyatt Earp Photo Page

http://www.ferncanyonpress.com/tombston/wyatt/photos. shtml

Maintained by Fern Canyon Press, this is a fascinating site that reproduces many photos of Earp, his family, and friends, as well as photos of related historical sites such as Tombstone in the lawman's era.

Wyatt Earp.net: Wyatt Earp History Page

http://www.wyattearp.net/

This site bills itself, probably truthfully, as "The Largest and Most Informative Wyatt Earp Site on the Net." It is maintained by author Steve Gatto.

PICTURE CREDITS

Page

INDEX

ABOUT THE AUTHOR

Adam Woog has written many books for adults, young adults, and children. He has a special interest in American history. Woog lives with his wife in Seattle, Washington, where he often visits Pioneer Square, the neighborhood where Wyatt Earp once ran a gambling concession.